A Native's Guide To Chicago's

SOUTH SUBURBS

by Christina Bultinck
and
Christy Johnston-Czarnecki

First Edition

Lake Claremont Press
4805 North Claremont Avenue
Chicago, Illinois 60625
http://members.aol.com/LakeClarPr

A Native's Guide To Chicago's South Suburbs
by Christina Bultinck & Christy Johnston-Czarnecki

Published June 1999 by:

Lake Claremont Press
4805 N. Claremont Ave.
Chicago, IL 60625
773/784-7517; LakeClarPr@aol.com
http://members.aol.com/LakeClarPr/

First Edition

ISBN: 0-9642426-1-3: $12.95 Softcover

Publisher's Cataloging-in-Publication
(Provided by Quality Books, Inc.)

Bultinck, Christina.
A native's guide to Chicago's South suburbs / by Christina Bultinck and Christy Johnston-Czarnecki. — 1st ed.
p. cm.
Includes index.
LCCN: 98-85577
ISBN: 0964242613

1. Chicago Suburban Area (Ill.)—Guidebooks. 2. Chicago Suburban Area (Ill.)—History. I. Johnston-Czarnecki, Christy. II. Title.

F548.68.B85 1999 917.73'110443
QBI99-327

Printed in the United States of America by United Graphics—an employee-owned company in Mattoon, Illinois.

To the memory of my grandmothers,
Dolores Bultinck and Loretta Laisch—
I hope I made them proud of me up there.

And to my family—
Grandpa Bultinck, Grandpa Laisch,
my parents Gabriel and Sandra,
my brother Gab, my sister Nikki,
Sam, and The Pipster
—CB

To my parents, James and Carol Johnston

To my husband Patrick and daughter Stephanie
—CJ-C

CONTENTS

Acknowledgments... vii

Introduction ...3

Alsip...9
Beecher...13
Blue Island...17
Bourbonnais...20
Calumet City...23
Chicago Heights...25
Crete...36
Evergreen Park...45
Flossmoor...47
Ford Heights...50
Frankfort...51
Glenwood...71
Harvey...75
Homewood...77
Joliet...85
Justice...101
Kankakee...103
Lansing...105
Lemont...107
Lockport...120
Matteson...131
Midlothian...140

Mokena...143
Monee...151
Morris...153
New Lenox...155
Oak Lawn...164
Olympia Fields...169
Orland Park...171
Palos Heights...177
Park Forest...180
Peotone...184
South Holland...189
Steger...191
Thornton...193
Tinley Park...199
Wilmington...211
Worth...213

Appendix A: Phone Numbers & Internet Addresses...215
Appendix B: Newspapers...220
Appendix C: Golf...223
Appendix D: Regional Maps...225

Bibliography...229
Index...233
Publisher's Credits...243
About the Authors...244

ACKNOWLEDGMENTS

We would like to thank everyone who helped us gather information to write this book. Pat yourself on the back if you are one of the following: research librarian; employee of a village hall, chamber of commerce, park district, cemetery, forest preserve, museum, or historical society; restaurant server; shop keeper; stranger who offered tidbits; family friend who gave input; or gas station attendant who put us on the "road to success." Thank you for taking the time to share information and leads. This book couldn't have been written without you. Thank you to every town listed in the book for putting up with our millions of questions. Also, thank you to Mary and Larry Rothenberg for their much appreciated information and friendliness. Thanks to Babe Seibrant for sharing her colorful family stories, and Phyllis Monks, P.C., of Crete for her contributions and time. Also, thank you to the crew at Balmoral Racetrack.

This book owes its existence to Lake Claremont Press and Sharon Woodhouse who conceived the brilliant idea of "exposing" the South Suburbs. I can't thank them enough for giving us the opportunity, the time (and boy, did we need time), and patience needed. We're forever grateful to Sharon and the whole crew at LCP: Brandon, Sue, Vikki, Bill, Ken, and everyone else that helped out.

Christina would like to personally thank:

My father, Gabriel, who picked up tabs, offered guidance on security issues, and lent me his car which racked up more miles than Happy Meals sold at McDonald's during a Furby promotion.

My mother Sandra and sister, Nikki, who I can't thank enough for spending countless hours gathering information on the history and architecture of each town. Their efforts as navigators, proofreaders, researchers, and chauffeurs will forever be appreciated and remembered.

My brother, Gab, Grandpa Bultinck, Grandpa Laisch, and family and friends who listened to me talk about nothing but work, work, work for the last year. They were all wonderful, understanding ego boosters who kept me going. Thanks!

Ms. Yos, my high school English teacher at Lincoln-way, who made me promise I'd become a writer and laughed at all my stupid jokes. All students should be so lucky as to have her as a teacher.

Last, but certainly not least, I need to thank Christy Johnston-Czarnecki, my co-author and best friend. She didn't run or scream when I asked her to join me on the project. She dove in, got to business, and helped create what I feel is the best guide to the South Suburbs. The fact that I was able to work with such a talented writer makes the project even more meaningful.

Christy would like to personally thank:

My husband Patrick, my beautiful baby girl Stephanie, and my parents James and Carol Johnston who taught me to always realize my dreams.

Mr. Yates, my senior high school English teacher, who believed in me when no one else did.

And, a very special thanks to my co-author Christina for having so much faith in my disorganized ways.

A Native's Guide To Chicago's

SOUTH SUBURBS

INTRODUCTION

Picture the South Suburbs in your mind. You know—that stretch of land past I-55. Chicagoans, and particularly Northsiders, probably envision a pot bellied man flipping burgers on the grill while wearing an open Hawaiian shirt, a stained white T-top underneath, and black socks up to his knees. Now, stop thinking of my boyfriend and really concentrate. Perhaps a young girl with braids running down a wheat-covered hill with a loyal dog at her side pops into your head. Wrong again, but kudos for remembering the opening to *Little House on the Prairie*. South-suburbanites probably picture their home town: green trees and fresh cut grass; the faint scent of someone's home cooking; the sound of birds chirping as the sun sets and reflects pink, orange, and purple off every surrounding window; children laughing and playing with no worries; ice cream trucks; running bases in the street; waving to your neighbors as they walk their dog and stop for a little conversation. Sounds nice doesn't it? This is what the South Suburbs are all about.

The peaceful South Suburbs, hereinafter referred to as SS, are truly a treasure in Illinois and I had always assumed that the residents of surrounding areas were aware of this. Not so. Soon after moving to Chicago I began dreading the question, "Where are you from?" because I knew the follow up would be, "Where's that?" The next five minutes would be spent trying to name a town relatively close that the person would know.

"Have you ever gone to the riverboats in Joliet?"
"No."
"Ever heard of Orland Park?"
"No."
"Do you know where you are right now (Chicago)?"
"Yes."
"I'm about 40 miles south."
"Oh, ok."

These conversations forced me to realize most non-SS residents have no clue what exists south of the city, and that their minds become a blank screen when trying to imagine what lurks there. Remember, the world is round, you will not fall off the planet if you set foot past I-55.

We hear the gossip. The Northern Suburbs and Chicago see themselves as admired, envied, and over ambitious and view the SS as uncultured, out-dated, slow, and altogether forgotten. Why are we looked down upon? It can't be because we're uneducated—we boast some of the best schools in the country. Also, some of the most expensive houses are located in the suburb of Frankfort. We can only conjure that Northsiders pay an insane amount of money for a house of equal size and craftsmanship to one in the SS, and to justify the expense they must label their area as "better."

Many people still think of the South and Southwest Suburbs as farm fields. They fail to realize the SS bear a colorful past and interesting, historical landmarks. Back in the 1600s when the region was known as New France, Joliet and Marquette had labeled it as some of the finest soil around. Most of the towns began in the early 1800s as small villages known for having the region's best soil. Washington Irving noted this natural bounty in his 1835 *Tour of the Prairie*,

> God has here, with prodigal hand, scattered the seeds of thousands of beautiful plants, each suited to its season, where there are no hands to pluck and few eyes to admire.

Today, more and more developers set their admiring eyes on the area, and more and more farmers sell their land to make way for new subdivisions and shopping plazas, thus making the broken down barns and towers icons of the area's agricultural past. As more people discover the beauty, transportation, recreation, and other resources that are available here, the SS finds itself in the midst of a boom. Fortunately, the larger these towns become, the tighter it seems the area hangs onto and preserves its history.

How do I know what town I live in?

Each town has its own section according to zip code. For example, Frankfort (60423) is made up of the Village of Frankfort, unincorporated Frankfort Square, Green Gardens, and Lincoln Estates. If you live in an unincorporated area and are confused about what town you fall under, take a moment to find an old bill or something with your address on it (we'll wait). Now, look at the town on the bill and locate it in the Table of Contents. Voilà. If you are still experiencing difficulties, please consult your local post office or move to one of the towns in the Table of Contents.

I'm from Chicago and have always been curious about the SS, but I don't want to do lots of traveling.

One exciting, advanced feature of the book is that we list the number of miles each town is from Chicago. This should break the misconception of the SS being "millions of miles" away from the city. In reality the SS are about 20-60 miles southwest of the city, and unless you travel by stagecoach, mule, or foot, you'll be here in a jiffy. Let's do some math. Homewood is 25 miles away. If a car leaves Chicago at 9 a.m. driving 50 m.p.h., what time will it arrive in Homewood? Depending on traffic, the answer is 9:30 a.m. It takes that long to get from Wrigley Field on Chicago's North Side to the LaSalle and Van Buren train station downtown. How about that! We just cut hundreds of thousands of miles off your commute and saved you a bundle in gas money—not to mention the wear and tear a million miles would have put on your car.

I'm directionless. How do I get there?

Major highways and roads that run through each town are listed. We created detailed road maps that will not only make us known worldwide as master cartographers, but will also serve as a handy travel guide. If you think you'll need more guidance, we recommend calling one of the numbers listed in the "contact numbers" section of each town before your first visit.

I'm from the SS and would like to know more about my local history.

Good for you for taking an interest in where you come from! How many nights have you watched Jay Leno asking people on the street simple historical questions to which they give absurd answers? It's horrifying! Benedict Arnold and Dolly Madison were chefs?! Paul Revere was British?! The American's fought Iraq in the Spanish-American War?! It's commendable when someone knows their country's past and doesn't take for granted how their region and country came to be what it is today. For this reason, we provide a historical background for each town. To truly appreciate each town you visit, you must be aware of the local history. We hope the many interesting historical facts we included about each town are just a starting point for your enjoyment of local history.

What have you done for us lately?

SS resources helped build pre-and-post-fire Chicago, made the Windy City the "Nation's Crossroads," provided the wood to build Chicago's first frame house, and the stone to build its Water Tower, Holy Name Cathedral, and Northwestern University. But, hey, the North Side *did* give us the Twinkie.

I can't get enough of Jeopardy.

Then you'll love the miscellaneous sections such as "Historical Landmarks", "We're #1, We're #1!", "Trivia", and "Famous Who's Who" scattered throughout the book. Spend hours of family fun learning about buildings on the National Register of Historical Places, firsts which occurred in the region, and miscellaneous trivia. Amaze friends and family with your abundant SS knowledge. Who knows? Maybe one day you'll be on Jeopardy and they'll have a "Chicago's SS" category. You'll be loving us then, won't you? Here's some pre-game show training for you. Hopefully after reading this book, you will be able to answer the following:

- Which town was a stop on the Chicago-Vincennes Pony Express Route?
- The community of Black Oaks has became known as what suburb?
- What community was named after the French-Canadian explorer who visited in 1673?
- Who haunts a particular stretch of Archer Ave.?
- At 1,235 feet, what is the highest point in the state?
- Miss America 1927 was from where?

- Fred MacMurray, star of "My Three Sons," was from what city?
- What city played in the 12th Annual Little League World Series?
- The Chicago Water Tower was built with stone from what town?
- Lionel Richie is from what town?

Is there anything to do in the SS?

The SS boasts award-winning restaurants, museums, art galleries, lakes, forest preserves, and much more! Check out the Entertainment sections for outdoor fairs, bars, dance clubs, arcades, and other fun stuff.

Are you taking donations for a "Liposuction Fund?"

Yes. We investigated eateries, restaurants, diners, cafes, supper clubs, pizza places, drive thrus, candy stores, and ice cream stands, believing it our duty, and honor, to eat everything possible in order to report to you on what's good and where to go. We put up with good service, bad service, too-darn-happy service, and "where is our service" service to assist you in the process. Is it unfair, then, to ask for donations to the "liposuction fund" or, at least, the "We need a new wardrobe because none of our clothes fit" charity? To make a donation, simply BUY MANY COPIES OF THIS BOOK.

I just bought a new pair of Birkenstocks and a backpack. Are there any peaceful nature walks or outdoor parks in the 'burbs?

The Touring sections lists ski paths, nature walks, bike trails, outdoor art, and murals, as well as old buildings and cemeteries with an interesting past.

What if I want to spend the night in the 'burbs? Do I have to sleep in my car at a rest stop?

Only if you want to. For all others, check out the Lodging sections, where you will find no-frills motels and installments of large hotel chains. All have indoor plumbing.

What if I want to buy a souvenir to prove I traveled to the South Suburbs?

Shopping remains a main activity in the SS, and the area has it all, from large malls and expansive flea markets to small and picturesque specialty stores. Antique fanatics may want to consider moving to the SS. You'll never want to leave once you've experienced the antique pickings in Lockport, Joliet, Lemont, Crete, and many other towns.

Is there anything you want to say to cover your butt?

Had we included every site, store, and restaurant located in the SS, you would now be the proud owner of the 15-volume set of *A Native's Guide to Chicago's South Suburbs.* We felt each town was worthy of a book dedicated solely to its own treasures, history, and resources. With 38 towns to cover (not including the unincorporated areas), however, we had to be selective in our reporting.

There are no doubt omissions and oversights which will occur to readers. We can only say that great effort was put forth over the last two years to do the best possible job and that updates of the book will include the new and different information we uncover in future explorations.

We are very proud to be able to bring this book to you and hope that in your time in the South Suburbs, you will experience what we have cherished there our whole lives.

ALSIP

Just The Facts

Village of Alsip
25 minutes from Chicago

Population:

1990	18,227
1995	13,705
2010	18,881

Contacts:
Village Hall 708/385-6902
http://www.lincolnnet.net/communities/alsip/alsip.htm

Access via:
I-94, I-57, I-80, and I-294

HISTORY

Alsip was first settled in the 1830s by Hanna and Joseph Lane. The name was derived from the Alsip Brickyard, which used to be in the area.

Although the current population of Alsip is under 20,000, the more than 750 industrial, retail, and commercial establishments located here bring the daytime population of Alsip to 40,000.

RECREATION

Alsip Park District
12521 S. Kostner
708/389-1003
The Alsip Park District was voted #1 in the nation and received the Gold Medal Award for excellence for providing outstanding leisure services to the community. Its Apollo Recreation Center operates a full size gymnasium, fitness center, whirlpool, and sauna. There's more! A four-acre aquatic park features a 285,000 gallon pool and includes two sand volleyball courts, horseshoe pits, a tanning hill, a washing pool, fountain, picnic area, and playground.

SHOPPING

Sanctuary Crystals
5524 Cal-Sag Road
708/396-2833
Want to cast a love spell on someone you have your eye on? What about performing a fast money spell for some quick bucks? Don't know where to start? Check out this store for all your magic needs. Not only a metaphysical bookstore, Sanctuary Crystal deals in stones, magical supplies, aromatherapy, jewelry, tapes, and global imports and sponsors monthly psychic fairs.
Open Mon. - Fri. 11 a.m. - 8 p.m., Sat. - Sun. 11 a.m. - 5 p.m.

Alsip, Home of the Dead?

Over the officials' dead bodies! In fact, one of the reasons this town incorporated was to avoid becoming a place for the permanently resting. Cemeteries were popping up so quickly in the area that there were concerns that the trend would continue unchecked. One of Alsip's first acts was to prohibit further cemetery expansion.

Dinah Washington, famous blues singer, is buried in Alsip's Burr Oak Cemetery. I wonder where her seven ex-husbands are buried?

Swap-O-Rama Flea Market
4350 W. 129th St.
708/344-7300
Swap-O-Rama, or as I call it Swap-ooooooooooooooooo-rama, and its hundreds of merchants epitomize wheelers and dealers. Permanent vendors, selling T-shirts, jewelry, herbs, spices, sports hats, Avon, Mary Kay, Beanie Babies, paintings, home decorations, kitchenware, purses, and oooooh so much more, ply their trade indoors. Since they will be at the market every week, it is advised to hit the outdoor area first. Temporary vendors vary from week to week and consist mostly of individual "garage sales" unloading comics, old books, furniture, ephemera, old records, clothes new and used, pottery, china, knick knacks, food, action figures, the hottest collectibles, artwork, electronics, car parts, tools, home supplies, and just about any other item you could hope for.

MAP OF BEECHER
N
W
E
S
CHURCH RD.
UP/CSX R.R.
ROMANS RD.
IL 1
WILLOW
CHESTNUT
CATALPA ST.
COUNTRY LN.
MEADOW LN.
ORCHARD LN.
MILLER ST.
MILLER ST.
SHADY LAWN GOLF COURSE
RACINE AVE.
DIXIE HWY.
FAIRWAY DR.
HODGES ST.
OAK PARK AVE.
ST.
ST.
ST.
REED ST.
ST.
BIRCH DR.
PENFIELD ST.
DUNBAR
ELLIOT
GOULD
WOODWARD
MAXWELL ST.
ELM
CATALPA ST.
INDIANA AVE
303RD. ST.
PASADENA AVE
BLOCK ST.
AHRENS DR.
CREST DR.
MELROSE LN.

BEECHER

Just The Facts

Village of Beecher
"A Proud Past and a Promising Future"
37 miles south of Chicago
(photo of Welcome to Beecher sign)

Land Area	3 sq. miles
Median Age	36
Median Family Income	$45,881
Average Sale Price of Home	$88,000

Population:

1990	2,032
1994	2,195
2010	2,612

Contacts:
Village Hall 708/946-2261
Chamber of Commerce 708/946-3145
http://www.lincolnnet.net/communities/beecher/beecher.htm

Access via:
Rt. 1 (Dixie Hwy.), Rt. 394 is just north and connects to 80, 94, and 294

HISTORY

The settlement of Beecher was prompted by a land grant offered by the Illinois Central railroad in the 1800s. By the time the Civil War had reached its peak, the land from the grant was sold. The village incorporated in 1884, the same year as the construction of the Home Life Insurance Building in Chicago—the world's first skyscraper. Originally known as The Center and then as Washington Center until 1870, a cattle herder named T.F. Miller changed the name to Beecher in honor of his preacher friend Henry Ward Beecher, the brother of Harriet Beecher Stowe, author of *Uncle Tom's Cabin.*

With a total land area of three square miles, Beecher is easy to drive right through and miss. Make an effort to stop for a visit or you will lose out on experiencing the friendliness, cleanliness, and security of a rare, small town.

TOURING

Beecher Library
673 Penfield
Located in the upper level of the Washington Township Building, this library houses a 1,500-square-foot, award-winning museum. Exhibits include railroad memorabilia and equipment, fire fighting gear, arms and armaments, and vintage clothing.

The large, brick building built in 1920 provides an attraction in itself. The front lawn displays a cannon from the Civil War that was donated by one of Beecher's early settlers.
Admission is free. Open Sat.

Gould Street is the historic highlight of Beecher.

Goodenow Grove Forest Preserve
27064 Dutton Rd.
Goodenow Grove offers 800 acres of hiking and biking trails, as well as a sledding hill and areas for ice skating, cross country skiing, picnics, and camping. Alcohol, children, and pets are allowed, however, children or pets drinking alcohol are not.
Open daily 8 a.m. - 8 p.m.

FOOD

Worthy of Serving a King or Queen

Princess Café
Located in the Olde Stage Tavern
502 Dixie Hwy.
708/946-3141
The large, multi-room restaurant, which today is known as the Princess Café, was originally the Old Stage Tavern and one of Beecher's first business establishments in the 1800s. Today it is a restaurant with a warm, supper club atmosphere and impeccable service.

Appetizing starters at Princess Café include Shrimp De Jonghe, sautéed shrimp, escargots en champignon, or the fried "hodge-podge" of mushrooms, zucchini, mozzarella sticks, and onion rings served with a marinara dipping sauce. Leave room for the relish tray of sweet pickles, scallions, celery, and carrots, which comes with a dip, a bowl of Swedish meatballs, and basket of bread. All entrees come with soup, salad, relish tray, and potato.

The roasted duck, one of the house specialties, comes with orange sauce and red potatoes splashed with garlic oil. Other excellent meals are the mushroom-topped filet mignon, the huge prime rib, Steak Diane, rack of lamb, pork chops, Athenian style chicken, Chicken Oscar, lobster tail, and frog legs. If it's not already obvious: you must eat here!
Entrees $14-$22. Reservations are recommended. Open daily 5 p.m. - 10 p.m.

Free P.O. Boxes

After hearing Beecher did not have postal delivery to much of the area, I visited the local office to inquire. Sure enough, it's true. Apparently, this is not so odd for a village of 3 square miles. Most residents pick up their mail at the local post office. However, they are given a post office box for free.

SHOPPING

Hidden Gem

Bultema Produce
29348 South Klemme Rd.
Bultema Produce is one of the best kept secrets of the South Suburbs. Besides fresh corn, tomatoes, peppers, cucumbers, herbs, and other vegetables at excellent prices, Bultema offers homemade barbecue sauce, breads, muffin mixes, salad dressings, pies, and specialties such as peanut butter marshmallow creme.

BLUE ISLAND

Just The Facts

City of Blue Island
"City on the Hill"
"Pride in our Past"
13 miles south of Chicago

Median Age	31
Median Family Income	$42,292
Average Sale Price of Home	$90,801

Population:

1990	21,103
1994	21,762
2010	19,622

Contacts:
City Hall 708/597-8600
http://www.lincolnnet.net/communities/blueisland/blueisland.htm

Access via:
I-57, I-80, I-57, and I-294

HISTORY

Blue Island began in 1835 as a way station for travelers along the Vincennes Trail. Blue Island was named after the blue vapor from the azure which the Indians saw when they looked over the hills.

Blue Island Trivia

The statue that appears at the opening of old Columbia films is Mrs. Jane Buckingham of Blue Island.

The **Joshua P. Young House** at 2445 High Street is on the National Register of Historic Places.

FOOD

Maple Tree Inn
13301 S. Olde Western
708/388-3461
If your mouth is watering for some New Orleans cooking get your butt over here! I do believe this is the only place in the SS to serve gumbo filled with oysters and alligator sausage. Don't leave without trying the Cajun martini! After you've had a few, be sure to hit the dance floor.
Call for reservations for groups of 8 or more. Open Tues. - Sat. 5 p.m. - 10 p.m. Closed Sun. - Mon.

Mario's Tacos
13325 W. Old Western Ave.
708/389-4023
Blue Island has a fast growing reputation as a town with great Mexican food, and Mario's Tacos can, in part, take credit for that acclaim. Their authentic recipes from south of the border include the peppers—eye-watering spicy, but oh, so good. Besides the usual Mexican fare like enchiladas, tostadas, tacos, and quesadillas, the menu also offers steak dinners and vegetarian plates.
Open daily 11 a.m. - 9:45 p.m.

SHOPPING

Midwest Stained Glass Arts and Repair
13019 S. Western Ave.
708/597-7972
Not just for your grandma anymore, stained glass is, and has been, a very trendy piece of artwork to own and display. This store's retail pieces are created by Sharon Kay Peterson, while associates Jack Hampton and Maurice Johnson do larger jobs such as homes and churches.
Open Mon. - Wed. & Fri. - Sat. 9 a.m. - 5 p.m., Thurs. 9 a.m. - 7 p.m. Closed Sun.

BOURBONNAIS

Just The Facts

Village of Bourbonnais

Access via:
Rt. 102, Rt. 113, I-55, and I-57

RECREATION

Kankakee River State Park was cherished first by Native Americans, later by traders and farmers, and, in the 1890s, by recreation seekers. Today, anglers, canoeists, hunters, campers, hikers, cyclers, and other outdoor enthusiasts find the park's recreational opportunities unsurpassed. The focus of the park is the Kankakee River which is listed on the Federal Clean Streams Register.

The Kankakee River area was being used by Illini and Miami Indians when the first Europeans made contact in the 1670s. By 1685 the Miami were sufficiently populous that the Kankakee River was called the River of the Miami. By the late 1600s to mid 1700s, Kickapoo and Mascouten entered the region followed by Potawatomis, Ottawas, and Chippewas.

The former site of the region's most extensive village, "Little Rock Village," is located inside the present-day park near the mouth of Rock Creek. In 1830 it was the site of the last great Indian Council. Most Potawatomi left the area by the end of the decade, except for Chief Shaw-waw-nas-see, whose grave is commemorated by a boulder along the nature trail at Rock Creek.

Fur traders Noel Le Vasseur, Hubbard Chabare, and Bourbonnais traded with the Potawatomi along the Kankakee and Iroquois rivers in the 1820s. When the Potawatomi left, Le Vasseur persuaded French Canadians to emigrate from Quebec to Bourbonnais, earning himself the title of "the father of Kankakee."

Hunting and Fishing

Kankakee River State Park has long been popular among hunters due to its abundant wildlife. Firearm hunting is permitted for duck, pheasant, woodcock, dove, rabbit, squirrel, fox, coyote, and raccoon; only bow hunting is allowed for deer.

Fishing enthusiasts can angle for the small mouth bass, channel catfish, walleye, and northern pike that are all in abundance in the Kankakee River. The park has two boat ramps for launching crafts with motors of ten horsepower or less.

Canoeing

815/932-6555
Call Kankakee River State Park Canoe Trips to reserve a rental canoe. Plan on a four or six-hour canoe trip to the park from the point of origination.

Camping

Kankakee River State Park has three separate camping areas. **Potawatomi Campground**, a Class A area, has 110 sites in a wooded setting. More than 150 sites are offered at **Chippewa Campground**, which has Class B electric, C, and D facilities. The **Horseback Campground** off Illinois Route 113 is open only from April 1st to August 31st. All areas require camping permits, which are available at the park office or from park personnel in state vehicles.

Trails

Hiking, biking, and cross-country skiing trails are on the river's north side, while horse and snowmobile trails can be found on the south side. A three-mile route along Rock Creek allows hikers to admire the beautiful canyons and waterfall.

Riding Stables

815/939-0309 (information)
Rent a horse at the park's riding stables on Deselm road, 3/4 of a mile north of Route 102. Guided horse rides, pony rides, hayrides, and cookouts all can be arranged at the stables.

CALUMET CITY

Just The Facts

City of Calumet City
"City of Homes"
25 miles south of Chicago

Contact:
City Town Hall 708/891-8100

Access via:
Calumet Expressway, I-394, I-80, I-57, I-294, I-94

TOURING

St. Andrew Church
155th and Lincoln Ave.
They don't make churches like this anymore! The Romanesque architecture, huge marble columns, marble saint statues, and 20-foot-wide stained glass windows make St. Andrew's (c. 1930)

We're #1! We're #1!

Lake Calumet and Calumet Harbor are the major ports for Chicago.

The Calumet River became a harbor in the 1860s when George Pullman decided to build his railcar factory on the west margin of Lake Calumet. The river was dredged from Lake Michigan to the docks Pullman built at his factory for shipping. It became a port when the Illinois legislature approved the creation of the Calumet Port District in the 1920s in order to provide Chicago with a second port (Navy Pier being the first).

a monument even Europeans would appreciate.

SHOPPING

We're #2! We're #2!
#2 Mall in the South Suburbs

River Oaks Mall
Managed by JMB Retail Properties Co.
96 River Oaks Dr.
708/868-0600
Half a million shoppers visit River Oaks Mall to shop in its 90+ stores, or catch a flick in their 14-screen theater. Major stores include Carson Pirie Scott, JC Penney, Marshall Field's, and Sears.
Open Mon. - Fri. 10 a.m. - 7 p.m., Sat. - Sun. 12 p.m. - 6 p.m.

CHICAGO HEIGHTS

Just The Facts

City of Chicago Heights
"Crossroads of the Nation"
27 miles south of Chicago

Median Age	30
Median household income	$33,098
Average Sale Price of Home	$61,600

Population:

1990	32,966
1994	33,713
2010	31,513

Contacts:
City Hall 708/756-5307
http://www.lincolnnet.net/users/lmchghts/

Access via:
Dixie Highway (IL. 50, Rt. 1), Lincoln Highway (U.S. 30), I-394, and I-294

HISTORY

Originally known as Thorn Grove, then Bloom, this South Suburb changed names more times than a black-listed writer, before it was finally incorporated as Chicago Heights in 1892. In the early 1900s Chicago Heights was a dominantly Italian neighborhood, but today its variety of homes and neighborhoods shows the growing financial and ethnic diversity of the area.

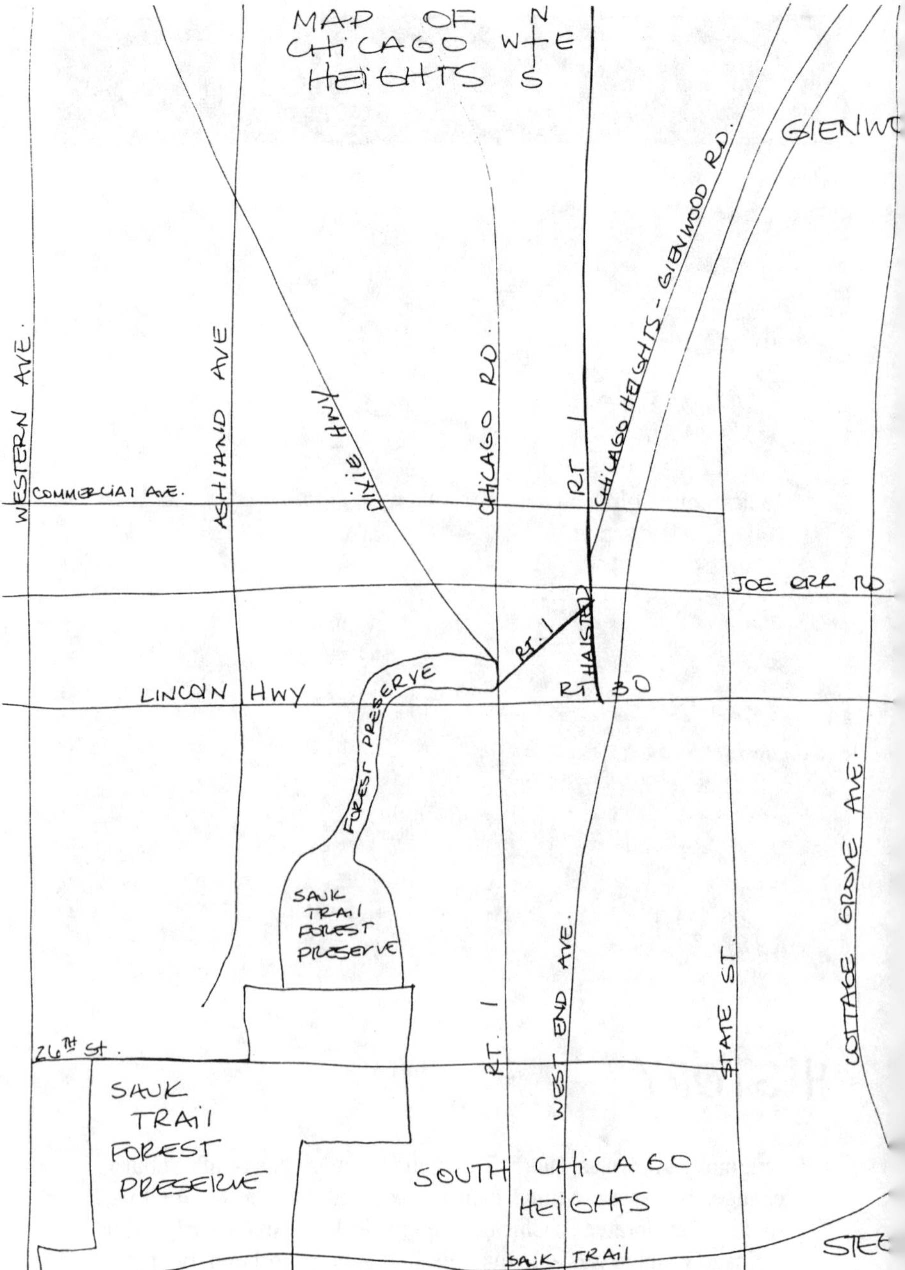

Chicago Heights

From 1930 to 1950, Chicago Heights became known as the "Crossroads of the Nation" due to the fact that transportation routes became more accessible and immigrants in search of employment flowed into the community of over 20,000 people. Today, Chicago Heights is the Southland's largest industrial center and home to Ford Motor Company's stamping plant, Calumet Steel, Rhone-Polanc, United Globe, Nippon, and Thrall Car.

On the National Register of Historic Places

Bloom Township High School
10th & Dixie Hwy.
WPA funds constructed the Bloom Township High School in 1934. The school boasts an international reputation for its architecture and six fresco murals. It also holds the honor of being the first suburban Chicago high school to be listed on the National Register of Historic Places.

TOURING

Some historical and architecturally stunning homes remain hidden in this city and are protected by the local Historic Preservation Advisory Committee. The city ordinance creating this committee states that Chicago Heights has "distinctive features in architecture, craftsmanship, landscape design, and cultural history thereby making it important to preserve, enhance, foster, and perpetuate these distinctive features as well as any future historic districts."

It's hard to look down a side street in Chicago Heights and not see a home being rehabbed in light of these lofty proclamations. Below are a few private residences that have completed their rehabbing:

- **149 W. Lincoln Hwy.** (a.k.a. 14th St. and Rt. 30)
  Corner of 14th (Rt. 30) and Schilling
  c. 1852
  The former home of pioneer banker William J. McEldowney is possibly the most publicized rehabbed home in the area, and rightfully so. The Victorian home is decorated for Christmas year round and is often mistaken for an antique store.

A rehabbed Victorian home at the corner of 14th and Schilling in Chicago Heights.

- **250 W. Lincoln Hwy.** (c. 1852)

- **Corner of Main St. and Euclid**

Another of Chicago Heights' many stunning rehabs sits on the corner of Main and Euclid.

We're #1! We're #1!

Payne Chapel, established in 1907, is the oldest continually existing church for African Americans in the country.

On October 13, 1916 the Conservation Committee of the Arche Club dedicated the Arche Fountain to mark the intersection of the first two trans-continental highways in the United States—Route 30 and Dixie Highway.

The Dante Club, an Italian men's club established in 1922, was said to be the only organization of its kind in the world. The club functioned as a social group that also helped immigrants assimilate into the American social structure.

Columbia Tool Steel (est. 1904) produced record amounts of tool steel for the production of war materials during World War II. In 1962 Columbia served as the prime supplier of dies used in fabricating parts for the Gemini space capsule.

American Brake Shoe and Foundry (est. 1902) was once considered the largest manganese foundry in the world.

Chicago Heights Who's Who in Sports

Brent Saberhagen, a Chicago Heights native, wears #17 as the starting pitcher for the Boston Red Sox. In 1985, he was voted World Series MVP and four years later he claimed the Cy Young and the American League ERA Leader awards.

Chicago Heights born Bryant Young plays defensive tight-end for the San Francisco 49ers and was part of the 1994 Super Bowl championship team.

Mike Prior went from Chicago Heights native to cheesehead when he became the safety for the Green Bay Packers.

Show a Little Respect

Bloomvale Cemetery
27th St. and East End Ave.
Now hidden under piles of trash and weeds, Bloomvale Cemetery accepted its last burial in 1912. This final resting site of roughly 339 early settlers will soon be dedicated as an official state landmark, but the trash and weeds have to be cleared first. If you're in the mood to do a good deed, show a little respect, and pick up some trash, the cemetery is located back in the trees, tangled with weeds.

The Battle of Chicago Heights
I don't know about you, but I find standing on ground that once belonged to a mass-murdering mobster pretty neat—especially if he belonged to the Capone gang. Chicago Heights is just one South Suburb in which you can do exactly that (not commit mass murders, but see where mobsters once hung out).

In the early 1920s to ward off other Italian beer-brewing competitors and annex the area as part of his empire, Al Capone sent Dominic Roberto, Jimmy Emery, and Frankie La Porte to seize control of Chicago Heights. **2606 Chicago Road**, now a parking lot, was home to Emery. La Porte lived at **212 East 22nd Street**, and Roberto lived at **2415 Chicago Road**, now an Amoco gas station. According to various accounts, Capone's gang was responsible for an outbreak of mysterious deaths which seemed to plague uncooperating competitors. After eliminating boss after boss of the Chicago Heights racket (about four) Al Capone had control of Chicago Heights's bars, speakeasies, gambling dens, and rackets. Historical books on the Capone gang cite "The Heights" as Capone's bootlegging refuge and arms depot.

Not many knew of Al Capone's association with "The Heights," or the loyal following of Italians there to protect him. Yet, the South Suburbs hold so many accounts of Capone hiding out in the area, that such stories have become legendary. Accordingly, reality evaporates and the myth becomes the truth.

FOOD

Free Food! Free Food!

The Tender Trap
109 S. Halsted
708/755-1134
The Tender Trap, a bar once known for it's dancing and game room, now serves food. That's right, salsa and chips for all from 4 p.m. - 6 p.m., making this is a good place to come and meet others who are also looking for free food. For those who don't mind forking over a little on Wednesdays, they serve snow crab legs or a 16-oz steak. Better yet, on Tuesdays, you can get a burger for a buck.
Open Sun. - Thurs. 11 a.m. - 2 a.m., Fri. - Sat. 11 a.m. - 4 a.m.

Best Place to Eat Breakfast

Egg & I
22 Dixie Hwy.
708/754-0909
Patrons constantly rave about Egg & I and it's impossible to get through a local Sunday paper without seeing an ad or write-up for this esteemed family restaurant. When you visit, you'll see why.

First of all, the entire restaurant is filled with the scent of freshly prepared pancakes. The prices are cheap (under $6/person), and the menu offers a wide variety of health-conscious meals. Two signature items include the Frittata (layers of egg, provolone cheese, onions, green peppers, chicken, and potatoes) and Crepeggs (crepes filled with eggs and choice of fillers).

The service exceeds our expectations, but you may also get the server who can hold entire conversations with herself about your dining needs and answer her own questions at a speed that could break the sound barrier. "Honey, how are you? You're good. Need coffee? No. Ketchup? Nah. Food OK? Of course it is. I'm just going to do two laps around the town and I'll be back to wipe your mouth." Well, maybe not that exactly, but close enough.

Add a varied menu, quick preparation time, a coffee cup that is never empty, and excellent food, and you'll know why we recommend

dining here.
Open Mon. - Sat. 6 a.m. - 3 p.m., Sun. 7 a.m. - 3 p.m.

Best Meatball in the World...Well, in The Southland

La Pergola
525 Dixie Hwy.
708/756-3737
This is known as one of the best Italian Restaurants in the South Suburbs, and not surprisingly, owner Joe DiSabato has been voted the best local chef in the area. He is also the creator of Sugo, his own special sauce, which can be purchased at the restaurant. Some menu items include baked clams, escargot, cavatelli with meatballs, rigatoni alla carbonara, prime rib, veal scallopine with spaghetti, lobster, baccala, mussels, zucchini parmigiana, bolognese, pizza, sandwiches, and some low calorie items.

The homemade gnocchi and Florentine soup I know first hand to be excellent, and I retain fond memories of a meatball that to this day, I talk about with anyone who will listen, and even a few who won't.

Though La Pergola has a children's menu, perhaps leave the kids at home for this one. The preparation and service take a little longer than usual (it's worth the wait), and you won't want crabby kids on your hands, the floor, or under the table when it comes time to enjoy the food.
Most entrees are $12-$18, but if you dine between the hours of 3:30 p.m. and 6 p.m. you can save $3-$4 off each meal. Delivery available. Open Fri. - Sat. 10 p.m. - 3 a.m., live entertainment Fri. - Sat. 10 p.m.

Aurelio's Pizza
708/481-5040
See description and hours under *Frankfort*, p. 58.

Amadio's Pizza and Pool Pub
Olympia Plaza
79 W. Joe Orr Rd.
708/754-4254
It looks small from the outside, but don't let that steer you away—there's plenty of room inside. For those who like to party until dawn,

Amadio's stays open until 4 a.m. and serves food until closing. To top that off, the pub opens up early enough for Sunday sporting events, when all beverages are half off. After 10 p.m. a DJ spins music from the 50s to the present. The menu includes pizza, calzones, and appetizers galore including, believe it or not, jalapeño poppers, wings, and breaded and fried veggies. Sandwiches, pastas, salads, and seafood are also available.
Open Mon. - Tues. 3 p.m. - 10 p.m., Wed. - Thurs. 11 a.m. - 11 p.m., Fri. - Sat. 11 a.m. - 12 a.m., and Sun. 11 a.m. - 12 a.m.

SHOPPING

Happiday Resale Mart
1207 S. Halsted
708/755-6464
At Happiday, you'll likely find a good selection of used books, games, and puzzles that are in decent shape; bed frames; cribs; lamps; old stereos; wall decorations; and art work. They also have clothes, shoes, knick-knacks, smaller appliances, dishes, jewelry, and records—all priced cheaper than usual thrift store prices. The employees work for free, and proceeds go to the Happiday School for the mentally challenged.
Open Mon. - Sat. 10 a.m. - 3:30 p.m. Closed Sun.

Second Chance II Resale Shop
417 W. 14th St.
708/481-4836
Second Chance carries the basic thrift store merchandise: books (Hardy Boys, Little Golden Books), records (of the sort that accompany Walt Disney picture books), clothes (infants, children, adults), etc. It's also a good store to check out if you're looking for appliances, wall clocks, picture frames, or trendier winter coats. A recent purchase was a cameo of Napoleon and Josephine Bonaparte in an intricately carved gold-tone frame for only $10. All proceeds go to the South Suburban Humane Society.
Open Mon. - Sat. 10 a.m. - 4 p.m. Closed Sun.

South Suburban Humane Society
1103 W. End Ave.
708/755-7387
Looking for a lost pet or one to adopt? Before viewing the ample selection of animals at the South Suburban Humane Society, everyone must fill out an application and show proof of identification. A sheet on each cage indicates the pet's name, age, how it arrived at the center, the gender, and if it has been spayed or neutered. I left feeling sad that I couldn't take Boomer, the black and white tabby, or Princess, the white Siamese cat, home with me. Maybe you can.
Open for adoptions/give aways Mon. & Wed. - Sat. 12 p.m. - 5 p.m. and adoptions only Sun. 1 p.m. - 4 p.m. Closed Tues.

SOUTH CHICAGO HEIGHTS

Just The Facts

Average Sale Price of Home $93,233

Access via:
IL 394

South Chicago Heights is a residential community with a small industrial base and a traditional downtown retail center. The latter is focused on the intersection of Sauk Trail and Dixie Highway, called "Brown's Corner." Local history relates that Adam Brown, the area's first white settler, built an inn on this spot.

FOOD

JoAnn's Hot Dogs & More
3101 Chicago Road
708/756-1522
At JoAnn's you can order to go, eat in, or zip through the drive-thru. Whatever your preference, you're in for some good chow! Menu items include five different hot dogs, Polish or Italian sausage sandwiches, tamales, fries, soup, and appetizers such as popper, chicken strips, cheese sticks, and the highly recommend Italian beef sandwich with hot peppers on a French roll.
Prices range from $.99 - $3.29, most under $2. Open Mon. - Fri. 10:30 a.m. - 7 p.m., Sat. 10:30 a.m. - 4 p.m. Closed Sun.

Sam's Restaurant
104 W. Sauk Trail
708/755-7100
A nice place to take the family or a group of friends for a casual meal (especially since the prices are very good for the amount of food served), Sam's offers your usual pastas, sandwiches, and appetizers. Most appetizers are deep-fried, but for the health conscious there's hot, soft bread with tomatoes. The specials are the menu's highlight—dishes like Chicken Oregano, T-bone steak, and roast pork tenderloin. All dinners come with bread, soup, salad bar, and potato or pasta.
Open Mon. - Fri. 11 a.m. - 11 p.m., Sat. 12 p.m. - 11 p.m., Sun. 12 p.m. - 10 p.m.

CRETE

Just The Facts

Village of Crete
30 miles south of Chicago

Land Area	6 sq. miles
Median Age	35.4
Median Family Income	$56,342
Average Sale Price of Home	$147,073

Population:

1990	6,773
1994	7,522
2010	11,693

Contact:
Village Hall 708/672-5431

Access via:
Rt. 1 (Dixie Hwy. / Main St.), I-80, 394, I-94, and 294

HISTORY

When real estate prices peaked in Chicago in 1836, an upstart named Willard Wood chose a site thirty miles south of the city to build a small log cabin. And proving that he was a true man of vision, he named that little log cabin Wood's Hotel.

After winning a seat in Congress in 1843, Long John Wentworth, a close friend of Mr. Wood's, established the first post office in the area. Willard Wood would become the first postmaster and then be assigned the task of naming the town. Taking this assignment very seriously Mr. Wood opened his Bible, saw the word "Crete" and, *boom*, the town was named. It incorporated some thirty years later in 1880.

Crete is an impressive town with beautiful new and old homes. The harness racing at Balmoral Park, quaint downtown antique shops, and six 18-hole golf courses make it a great place to spend the day.

Making a wrong turn in Crete, however, may put you smack in the middle of farmland as far as the eye can see. If you're directionless or don't own one of those nifty compasses in your car, a good landmark to head for is the old Lincoln Fields Water Tower on Rt. 1. According to some stories, Capone's gang developed a prehistoric form of off-track-betting at the tower. It is said that while some of Capone's gang members were watching the races at the racetrack (now Balmoral Park), Capone was taking bets from atop the tower.

Build It and They Will Come...or Maybe Not

Hattendorf Hotel
c. 1892
Henry Hattendorf, positive that the overflow of crowds at the 1893 World's Columbian Exposition in Chicago would seek lodging south of the city, erected a hotel off the Chicago & Eastern Illinois Railroad line. Unfortunately for him, Chicago's Palmer House and Old Hyde Park Hotel were closer to the fair's Hyde Park location. Nonetheless, his grand structure possessed four levels, a ballroom which occupied the entire third level, thirteen bedrooms and one bath on the second floor, and ten rooms on the first floor. He built it, but no one came, and in 1964 his field of dreams was destroyed.

RECREATION

Balmoral Woods Country Club
26732 S. Balmoral Woods Dr. (across from Balmoral Park)
708/672-7448
The site of the 1991 U.S. Open qualifying rounds, this 18-hole

championship course cuts through 10,000 oak trees. All rates include a cart.
Weekdays $35, $30 after 3 p.m. Weekends $45, $38 after 4:30 p.m. Opens Mon. at 8 a.m., Tues. - Fri. at 7 a.m., and Sat. - Sun. at 5:30 a.m. Hours vary, so phone first.

Lincoln Oaks Golf Course
390 Richton Rd.
708/372-9401
Lincoln Oaks is a public, 18-hole course that previously hosted the IPGA Assistant Championship and U.S. Open qualifier.
Weekday rates run $18 before 3 p.m. and $10 after that, with a special senior rate of $9.50. Weekends are $18.50 before 10 a.m., $25 until 3 p.m., and $13 thereafter. Open year round.

ENTERTAINMENT

Once the Most Modern Horse Racing Track in America

Balmoral Race Track
26435 S. Dixie Hwy.
708/672-7544
In 1925 Colonel Matt J. Winn, originator of the Kentucky Derby, came to Chicago to survey the racing scene. The South Suburbs of Chicago impressed him, and on August 9, 1926 he made Crete the site of his Lincoln Fields racetrack (Balmoral since 1955). Stuyvesant Peabody, Sr., president of Peabody Coal Company and a descendant of one of the wealthiest families in Illinois, was among the early investors, and Marshall Field, founder of Field's Department Store, was an early director.

Today the park displays photos of guests from the 1920s enjoying a day at the park. The same train depot they flooded to enter and leave the station is only a skeleton and a memory today.

Some jockeys who have raced at Balmoral Park over the years and are now in the National Hall of Fame include Earl Sande, John Adams, George Woolf, Steve Brooks, Tommy Burns, and Eddie Arcaro. Amelia Earhart, Diamond Jimmy Moran, Tom Duggan, George Steinbrener (George!), and Lou Boudrow as well as other celebrities have attended the park. Here's an "Earhart" theory for you: Maybe Amelia was doing some OTB by the watertower with Capone and failed to pay a debt. Do you think Capone's gang might have rigged her plane as payback? Remember that you heard it here first. Some of the excitement of Balmoral was captured on screen in the scenes from the movie *Sting* that were filmed here.

Today the park hosts special races such as Super Night, which is the best of the best in thoroughbred racing and features more than 1.2 million in prizes. About once a month, Balmoral holds a "special night" with many giveaways. Some past prizes include snowmobiles, go carts, jet skis, weekend packages, and Lazy Boy recliners. The park also holds raffles for free parties that allow winners to invite 25 friends to the track for 1-1/2 hours of free beer, wine, pop, and food.

Besides thoroughbred racing and OTB, Balmoral hosts The Crete Antique Expo and Crete Art Fair each year. This is in addition to a slate of 50s dances, concerts, fairs, walkathons on the track, picnics, weddings, and company outings that are held there. The VIP room has it own bar, pool table, and makes a great site for a bachelor/ette party.

You've taken in a lot of information here, so let us sum this up into two sentences: Balmoral Park is the answer to your "What are we doing tonight?", "I don't know what do you want to do?", "I don't know what do you want to do?" conversations. They have great food, beautiful views, intriguing history, and excitement. Who knows, may-be you can put some extra green in your pocket too?
Open Mon. - Sun. 11 a.m.- 11 p.m. Racing Tues., Fri., & Sat.; OTB Mon., Wed., Thurs., & Sun. Grandstand admission is free, the 2nd floor is $2, the dining room is $2 with a $5 minimum order.The park has a seating capacity of 12,000 and a typical Sat. crowd of 2,000-2,500.

FOOD

Slam or Sip. A Bonding Experience Either Way.

The Coffee Cottage, Inc.
1407 Main St.
708/672-0682

Upon entering the friendly Coffee Cottage, I knew fate had drawn me to one of the trendiest spots in Crete. A bar area lines the front entrance for patrons who want to slam the caffeine and go. To them, I suggest one of the five daily blends. A small, ten-ounce cup can be consumed in less than five minutes. (As with any establishment that mainly deals in caffeine, this cottage has a fast-paced, bustling atmosphere.) For those who adopt a slower pace in life and can't fathom sipping a cup of coffee in less than 45 minutes, The Coffee Cottage accommodates with huge, green couches and various tables and chairs. (The lingering crowd seems to be made up mostly of mothers and daughters.) Go for a cappuccino, espresso, cafe mocha, latte, or one of the many flavored teas.

Open Mon. - Thurs. 6 a.m. - 8 p.m., Fri. - Sat. 6 a.m. - 9 p.m., Sun. 6 a.m. - 4 p.m.

Onion Ring Capitol of the WOOOOOOOOOrld

Cal's Chicken City, U.S.A.
1412 Main St.
708/672-9299

For late risers, Cal's is considerate enough to serve breakfast until 2 p.m. The log cabin interior look is reminiscent of Paul Bunyon's in Wisconsin. Sandwich choices include beef, corned beef, sausage, reubens, steak, and chicken sandwiches—among about twenty others—all priced between $1.45 and $6.25. Every vegetable one could hope for comes battered and deep fried. Fried chicken comes in many "packages" and runs from $1.99 to $14.25. Fixin's such as slaw, fries, and 'tatos are extra ($.79-$2.50). The menu declares they are the onion ring capitol of the world, and I'll back up their claim.

Open Sun. - Thurs. 7 a.m.- 9 p.m., and Fri. - Sat. 7 a.m.- 10 p.m.

Chuck's Place
1358 Main St.
708/672-9449
Yet another hopping place in the heart of downtown Crete. Perhaps the dominantly male crowd at Chuck's are all the husbands and brothers of the mothers and daughters at the Coffee Cottage. On any given night or weekend day this bar is jam packed with Creteians. Some highlights of the menu of appetizers and sandwiches are the mini chicken tacos, the hoagies, the Krakus ham and cheese, and the pork chop sandwich.
Open Mon. - Fri. 11 a.m - 11 p.m., Sat. 11 a.m. - 5 p.m., Sun. 11 a.m. - 8 p.m.

Another Bunyon Flashback

Northwoods Saloon
968 E. Steger
708/672-1167
As the name may hint, Northwoods Saloon has a woodsy appeal and resembles a tavern set deep in the heart of Canada. The stone fireplace, log cabin look, and stuffed animals on the walls (and we're not talking Beanie Babies) create a warm, cozy feel.

Delicious and hearty food matches the atmosphere: Appetizers include chicken logs (chicken, cheese, and red peppers wrapped in tortilla shells) and homemade bread with a side of Wisconsin cheese. Perch and chicken breast with mushroom gravy are among the tastiest entrees, especially when paired with homemade mashed potatoes topped with green onions, bacon, Cheddar, sour cream, and butter. Those same potatoes are also the main ingredient in the baked potato pie. Sandwich options such as bratwurst, pot roast, beef with provolone, smoked ham and provolone, and turkey with bacon and Swiss round out the satisfying culinary lineup.
Entrees $5.45 - $21.95, sandwiches $5.25-$7.25, appetizers $1.75-$6.25. Open Mon. - Sun. 11 a.m. - 10 p.m.

Brauhaus
1381 Benton
708/672-6864
The Brauhaus offers dinners ($6.95-$19.95) like liver with apple and onion, spiesbraten, wiener schnitzel, and huhn (chicken) schnitzel, accompanied by potato pancakes and soup or salad. For those of you

who go to ethnic restaurants only to order American, the Brauhaus offers ½ lb. Hamburgers for $1.95 on Mondays, all-you-can-eat fried chicken for $7.95 on Wednesdays, and all-you-can-eat Alaskan white fish for $6.95 on Fridays. Appetizers ($4.95 - $6.95) such as bean soup, cheese sticks, mushrooms, and chicken wings are almost a meal in themselves.
Open Mon. - Sat. 11 a.m.- 11 p.m.

Best Pizza

Aurelio's Pizza
1372 Main St.
708/672-4000
See description under *Frankfort*, p. 58.
Open Sun. - Thurs. 11 a.m. - 10 p.m., Fri. 11 a.m. - 12 a.m., Sat. 11 a.m. - 12: 20 a.m.

SHOPPING

Ewe & Me
500 Fifth St.
708/672-6499
Ewe & Me is the ultimate country craft store. No need to make a trip to Wisconsin's prized Door County when you have all the "crafty-homemade" stuff right here in the SS. A "kitchen" displays antique furniture, stoves, pottery, pans, cups, and utensils, along with homemade jams and butters (cherry, peach, and pumpkin). Further into the store is a large selection of handmade teddy bears, bunnies, and elephants—all in cute outfits, handmade candles, and other folk art items.
Open Tues. - Fri. 10 a.m. - 5 p.m., Sat. 10 a.m. - 4 p.m.

Wee Folks Peddlers
1344 Benton St.
708/672-6590
Wee Folks peddles Boyd's bears, cards, gifts, dried floral designs, folk art, painted furniture, reproduction furniture, and other wares for the home.
Open Tues. - Sat. 10 a.m. - 5 p.m.

Best Store Display in Crete

Gatherings
1375 Main St.
708/ 672-9880
At first it may seem like you're in a *Twilight Zone* episode starring as Martha Stewart trapped in *Country Living* magazine. At second glance, you will be assured that you're in Gatherings—the "cutest" store in Crete and one of the best in the South Suburbs. For those looking to redecorate with the stylish looks seen on the covers of the decorating and country magazines, this is the place to go. However, the bedroom, kitchen, bathroom, and sun room displays set up in almost museum fashion make one hesitate to pick up a piece of merchandise. Antique carts hold Limoges china in mint condition; the bathroom display features handmade soaps, antique bottles, and gifts such as artist-made jewelry and clothing. Other great products are the trendy country furniture hutches, bureaus, nightstands, bed sets, and antique glass.
Open Tues. - Sat. 10 a.m. - 5 p.m., Sun. 12 p.m. - 5 p.m.

Teryl's Boutique
1406 S. Main St.
708/672-8778
Teryl's designer clothing boutique carries a wide variety of silk clothing, plus purses, scarves, Austrian crystal jewelry, and, for those who long to look more intelligent, designer non-prescription glasses. A ribbed silk, button-down sweater for $29 is a typical good find.
Open Mon. - Wed. & Fri. - Sat. 10:30 a.m. - 5 p.m., Thurs. 10:30 a.m. - 7 p.m., Sun. 12 p.m. - 3 p.m.

Indian Wheel Co.
1366 Main St.
708/672-9612
Did you ever have an elderly relative who collected everything, and walking into their home was candy for the eyes because there were "things" to look at in every square inch of the house? Indian Wheel Co., one of the largest antique stores on the South Side, will remind you of that house. The walls, cabinets, and floor are filled with salt and pepper shakers, political buttons, illustrated children's books, furniture (like whole kitchen sets), radios, toys, and much more.
Indian Wheel Co. also purchases items and conducts estate sales.
Open Tues. - Sat. 10 a.m. - 5 p.m., Sun. 12 p.m. - 5 p.m.

SPECIAL EVENTS

Wild West Days
Crete Park
515 First St.
708/672-6969
Mid-August
Enjoy reenactments of the Old West as well as arts and crafts booths and costume contests.

Christmas House Walk
708/672-3369
First weekend in December
For ten years, five historic homes in Crete literally "deck the walls" for the self-guided annual Christmas house walk. The night sky is lit up by the Country Christmas parade, the highlight of the evening.

EVERGREEN PARK

Just The Facts

Village of Evergreen Park
"Village of Churches"

Population:

1990	20,874
1994	21,024
2010	20,014

TOURING

St. Mary Cemetery & Mausoleum
87th St. and Pulaski Rd.
708/422-8720
Est. 1888
St. Mary's is resting place to football player Brian Piccolo.

FOOD

Best Ribs

Roll'n Ribs
8715 S. Kedzie
708/425-2585
Noses, taste buds, and stomachs will all be hypnotized by the aroma coming from Roll'n Ribs. The distinct flavor and aroma of the house sauce come from apple wood, which the restaurant uses instead of hickory or mesquite like most other ribs places.
Open Sun. - Thurs. 11 a.m. - 9 p.m., Fri. - Sat. 12 p.m. - 10 p.m.

Souzy's Drive-In
3801 W. 95th St.
708/423-0166
Souzy's is a cute little drive-in off busy 95th Street, whose menu offers a variety of treats from burgers and chili to ice cream. The homemade chili, the Souzy Burger, and the Spanish Burger are highly recommended. Some of the best in the SS, the sweet and spicy chili can clear sinus congestion in seconds! The Spanish burger's unique taste comes from layers of green olives.
Open Mon. - Sat. 11 a.m. - 7 p.m. Closed Sun.

Famous Who's Who

Among the graduates of Evergreen Park Community High School is "Unabomber" Ted Kaczynski. Other notable alumni include former White Sox pitcher Don Pall, Grammy winner Jim Yukich, and journalist Morton Kondracke, known for conducting the last interview with former President Richard Nixon.

FLOSSMOOR

Just The Facts

Village of Flossmoor
25 miles south of Chicago

Access Via:
Calumet Expressway (I-94), the Tri-State Tollway (I-80/94), I-57, and U.S. Route 30

HISTORY

Chicago purchased Flossmoor in 1890 to use its dirt to prepare for the 1893 Columbian Exposition. Unfortunately, the dirt, not Grade A, wasn't fit to be used and the area was slated for development instead. A contest soon followed to name this acreage of inferior dirt. "Flossmoor," meaning "dew on the flowers" in Gaelic, won out with its delicate reconstruction of the land's image.

Beginning its destiny as a golfer's paradise, Flossmoor quickly became a summertime escape for wealthy Chicago businessmen in the 1920s. Their affluence remains preserved in Flossmoor's elegant mansions, residential areas, and stores. Street names like Caddy, Bunker, and Brassie reflect the area's early creation of some of the finest golf courses to be found anywhere. It's impossible to go through this town without seeing a license plate that reads "EZ Par 4" or the like.

Trivia

For a taste of Frank Lloyd Wright's work, visit 1136 Brassie Ave.

In 1969, Homewood and Flossmoor merged their park districts and now maintain over 200 acres, 30 parks, a racquetball/fitness club, ice skating arena, lake, and other centers. In 1991 these combined park districts won the National Gold Medal Award from the National Sporting Goods Association.

Golf courses are what this town is known for—prestigious, manicured, professional golf courses. Among them are:

- **Flossmoor Country Club** (1441 S. Western, 708/798-4700), one of the oldest and most prestigious in the area.

- **Idlewild Golf Club** (19201 Dixie Highway, 708/798-0514), a private club that has hosted thousands of golfers and tournaments on the professional circuit since its 1908 establishment, and

- **Cherry Hills Golf Country Club** (100 91st at Kedzie, 708/799-5600), winner of "Best of Chicago Southland" awards. *9 holes are $11 during the week and $13 on the weekend ($12 extra for a cart). 18 holes run $21 ($22 extra for a cart) during the week and $27 ($26 extra for a cart) on the weekends.*

RECREATION

Iron Oaks
2453 Volmer Rd.
708/481-2330
The 33-acre Iron Oaks nature preserve is a joint project of Olympia Fields and Homewood-Flossmoor. Outdoor enthusiasts can enjoy a variety of activities here, such as hiking and skiing. The main attractions are the prairie restoration, which includes a pond and marsh area; the native prairie plants garden; and the experimental educational course that consists of a 35-foot rope course and a 50-foot climbing tower.

FOOD

Fresh Starts Restaurant and Bakery
1040 Sterling Avenue
708/957-7900
Fresh Starts' menu changes with the seasons. This unique restaurant features a specialty bakeshop, custom catering, espresso bar and full service liquor bar. Some items from their Spring/Summer menu include pan seared scallops, lobster ravioli, and Dijon lamb for appetizers; entrees of filet mignon, Thai chicken, stuffed pork tenderloin, and potato lasagna; and citrus marinated chicken, Carolina BBQ Pork, and carving board turkey club sandwiches.
Appetizers $5.95-$8.95, sandwiches $5.95-$6.95, entrees $12.95-$23.95. Open Mon. 7 a.m. - 4: 30 a.m., Tues. - Thurs. 7 a.m. - 9 p.m., Fri. 7 a.m. - 10 p.m., Sat. 8 a.m. - 10 p.m.

Flossamore Italian Market, Inc.
2550 Central Drive
708/922-2667
Visiting Flossamore Italian Market in downtown Flossmoor is like a trip to Old Italy. The owners have re-created the Old Italian neighborhood grocery, complete with imported lunchmeats and cheeses, unique gift items, and homemade specialties.
Open Mon. - Fri. 10 a.m. - 7 p.m., Sat. 9 a.m. - 6 a.m.

FORD HEIGHTS

Just The Facts

Village of Ford Heights
30 miles south of Chicago

Contact:
Village Hall 708/758-3131

HISTORY

The area now called Ford Heights was a station on the Underground Railroad prior to the Civil War. In 1949 it incorporated under the name Ford Heights, chosen because of its location East of Chicago Heights and near the Ford Motor Company factory.

FRANKFORT

Just The Facts

Village of Frankfort
"The Community with 1890s charm"

Land Area	9.25 sq. miles
Median Age	37.3
Median Household Income	$75,071
Average Sale Price of Home	$181,537

Population:

1990	7,180
1994	7,863
2010	20,643

Contacts:
Village Administration 815/469-2177
Chamber of Commerce 815/469-3356
http://www.lincolnnet.net/frankfort.vil/

Access via:
I-80, U.S. Rt. 30, and U.S. Rt. 45

HISTORY

Although settlers from other countries came first, German immigrants grabbed a hold of Frankfort and made it their home away from home. In the 1840s, German settler Frederick Cappel literally made it his home away from home when he slapped the label of his native city, Frankfurt-am-Main, on the town. That name stuck until 1855

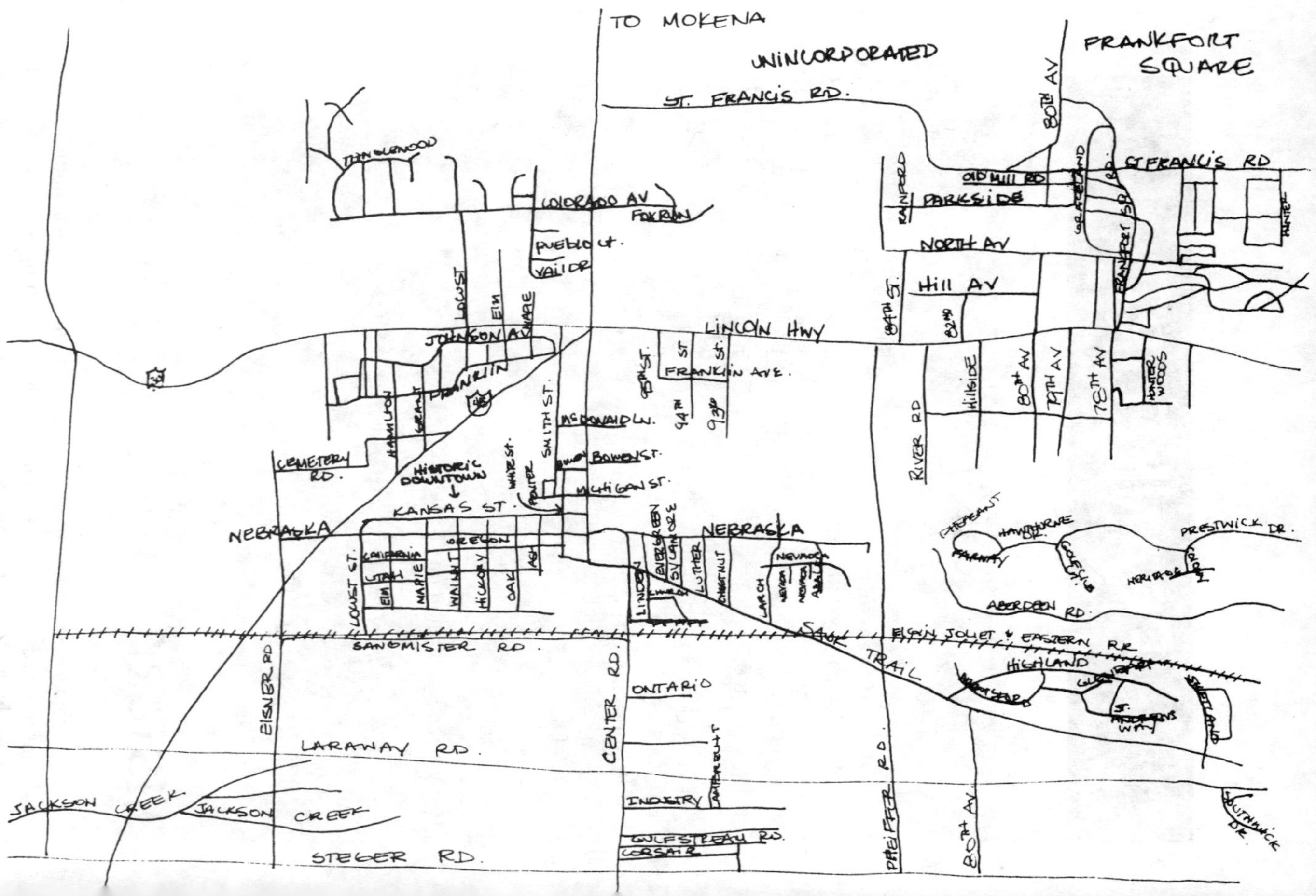
TO MOKENA
UNINCORPORATED
FRANKFORT SQUARE
ST. FRANCIS RD.
80TH AV
ST FRANCIS RD
OLD MILL RD
PARKSIDE
RANFORD
NORTH AV
HILL AV
84TH ST.
82ND
LINCOLN HWY
HILLSIDE
80TH AV
79TH AV
78TH AV
HUNTER WOODS
RIVER RD
COLORADO AV
FOXRUN
PUEBLO CT.
VAIL DR
LOCUST
ELM
WARE
JOHNSON AV
FRANKLIN
HAMILTON
GRANT
CEMETERY RD.
HISTORIC DOWNTOWN
SMITH ST.
WHITE ST.
McDONALD LN.
BOWEN ST.
MICHIGAN ST.
KANSAS ST.
NEBRASKA
CALIFORNIA
UTAH
ELM
MARIE
WALNUT
OREGON
HICKORY
OAK
ASH
LOCUST ST.
FRANKLIN AVE.
94TH
93RD
LINDEN
EVERGREEN
SYCAMORE
LUTHER
CHESTNUT
LARCH
NEVADA
HAWTHORNE DR.
FAIRWAY
GOLF CLUB
HERITAGE
PRESTWICK DR.
ABERDEEN RD.
ELGIN JOLIET & EASTERN R.R.
SAUK TRAIL
HIGHLAND
ST. ANDREWS WAY
SUNTLAND
SANGMISTER RD.
EISNER RD
CENTER RD.
ONTARIO
LARAWAY RD.
INDUSTRY
GULFSTREAM RD.
CORSAIR
JACKSON CREEK
JACKSON CREEK
STEGER RD.
PFEIFFER RD.
80TH AV
SOUTHWICK DR.

Frankfort

when the Joliet and Northern Indiana Railroad named it Frankfort Station. The "Station" was dropped 24 years later upon incorporation.

Frankfort's skillful restoration of its historic downtown district shaped it into one of the most desirable places in the SS to shop and dine.

To clearly picture Frankfort, imagine an archery target: the outer circle is full of beautiful, untouched, tree-scaped land complete with a flowing creek. Large newer homes, shopping complexes, and bustling business plazas comprise the inner rung, which encompasses the center of town, Kansas Street—a well preserved historic district with beautiful, pre-Civil War homes and buildings. One would almost think that time stood still for downtown Frankfort as the world built around it. No wonder it is considered the "Jewel of the Southland."

Within the past ten years, Frankfort's population has nearly tripled, making it one of the fastest growing communities in all of Northern Illinois.

TOURING

Historical Landmarks

The Grainery
Corner of Elwood and Oak
The grain elevator dubbed "The Grainery" has long been a part of the South Suburban landscape.

Historic Downtown Frankfort
Bounded by Kansas St., White St., Maple St., and Utah St.
Listed on the National Register of Historic Places, Kansas Street in downtown Frankfort is a walk back in time and a great place to shop. For a narrated audio tour through downtown Frankfort, stop into **Always Open** (6 Elwood St., 815/469-7270) or the **Frankfort Historical Museum** (132 Kansas St., 815/469-6541) for a tape and

Cemeteries

Union Cemetery
Green Garden Township
This abandoned German cemetery, with burials dating back to 1856, is the only remaining evidence of a German Baptist Church that was built prior to 1861. Civil War soldier Private V.H. Hinrichs, Co. C 100 Ill. Inf. is buried here.
Not open to the public.

Pleasant Hill Cemetery
Off Elsner Road between Nebraska and Brookside Lane
Before written records of the cemetery were kept, wooden grave-markers were the only means of identification at Pleasant Hill. These have long since decayed, which makes dating the first burial impossible. However, there are 14 Civil War soldiers buried here.
Open dawn to dusk.

Rose Hill Cemetery
Stuenkel Rd. between Center Rd. and Rt. 45
Green Garden Township
When one is touring a cemetery, the lure is often the history and architecture of the monuments. Besides the towering Virgin Marys, the first headstones to usually catch one's eye are the unreadable, white limestone graves: they certainly give off an air of mystery about who is buried there. Such is the appeal of this small German cemetery, which is lined with less than a dozen rows of marble and limestone graves that date back to the 1800s and are barely legible.
Open dawn - dusk.

The 1891 grave of a 4-year-old at Frankfort's Rosehill Cemetery.

Unincorporated Frankfort, where old farm buildings are still an important piece of the landscape.

tape recorder. The half-hour tour is free, but there is a $3 refundable deposit.

Victorian horsedrawn carriage tours are offered year round by **Jim and Becky's Horse and Carriage Service** (708/534-7600). They are on hand every Sunday in downtown Frankfort for the Concerts on the Green (June - August). Tours begin at $15 for four people to ride ten minutes around the historic district. For $15 more, the carriage tours the older adjoining subdivisions as well as the historic district.

The Frankfort Historical Museum
132 Kansas St.
815/469-6541
See what life has been like for residents of Frankfort from its early settlers to its present-day inhabitants. Great displays of local history include three large window exhibits (changed regularly) depicting historic scenes from the area. A barbershop, home, and general store are some of the museum's past re-creations.
Open Sun. 1 p.m. - 4:30 p.m.

Here Today Gone Tomorrow

Alsip Nursery
North on Rt. 45
A familiar site while driving north on Rt. 45 by Alsip Nursery is a small, white wooden gazebo and matching picnic tables. The foliage, trees, and tall grass are now the only dwellers on this former site of many celebrations prior to the 1940s. Some of the trees surrounding

the area are 250 to 400 years old. You probably never paid much attention to it before, nor do you probably know that a similar site sat on the land which Alsip Nursery now stands. Admire it while you can: it has already been purchased by a developer and will soon be the site of a new subdivision.

RECREATION

Frankfort Bowl and Billiards
15 S. Ash St.
815/469-5333
When local residents don't want to go far, but they want to go somewhere, they hang out at Frankfort Bowl and Billiards. The owners gave it a new look a few years ago and decked it out with black and white checked floors that give it a 60s look and feel. When you enter you will see the pool tables, dartboards, tables, jukebox (stocked with choice 80s songs), and bar. To the left are TVs, pinball, and video games. In the back through a doorway is the always-packed bowling alley.
Open Tues. - Fri. 6 p.m. - 1 a.m., Sat. 1 p.m. - 1 a.m., Sun. 3 p.m. - 10 p.m.

Green Garden Country Club
Manhattan-Monee Rd. and Center Rd.
815/469-3350
Green Garden Country Club offers a tranquil getaway amidst a beautiful country backdrop. Rates for 18 holes during the week are $25 or $13 for senior citizens. Twilight rates (after 3 p.m.) are $22 with a cart or $14 to go by foot. Weekend rates are slightly higher with 18 holes at $32. If you're just starting out or need some refresher tips, the club offers lessons at $50 per hour.

The club's beautiful, window-lined dining room allows patrons to enjoy a hearty meal while keeping an eye on the competition. The week-end breakfast buffet offers individually-made omelettes, crepes, pancakes, French toast, bagels, fruit, bacon, sausage, and other breakfast items.
Open year round.

ENTERTAINMENT

Lincoln-Way Theater Guild
815/464-7079
The guild performs various shows, such as the recent *Pump Boys and Dinettes*, at the Trolley Barn in downtown Frankfort.
Tickets run about $12. Open Mon. - Thurs. 4 p.m. - 9 p.m.

Concerts on the Green
Corner of Kansas and White St.
815/469-3356
In the months of June, July, and August, Frankfort hosts Concerts on the Green on Breidert's Green (the old train station in downtown Frankfort by the Grainery). Bring a blanket and food for a little picnic, and you're set for a relaxing Sunday evening under the stars—unless, of course, it rains. Never fear, the concerts are moved into the Trolley Barn during inclement weather.

FOOD

Hey Jagermeister!

Die Bier Stube
42 Kansas St.
815/469-6660
Do you ever get an urge to have the Yodeler from the *Price is Right* stand before you in his green knickers and bow tie, serenade you with German songs, and command you to do shots of Jagermeister? Well, it won't be a personal songfest, but at Die Bier Stube, two Yodeler look-alikes, Johann and Peter, play the accordion and sing energetic songs for the entire crowd, stopping often to down a shot or take a swig with everyone. Besides their uncanny resemblance to the Yodeler, the tolerance level of these men is amazing!

Truly a genuine German restaurant right down to the servers' costumes, the entertainment adds a finishing element of ethnicity to Die Bier Stube. The European decor of stuffed pheasants, bear, steins, plates, military memorabilia, cuckoo clocks, and more will keep your

eyes busy. For dinner, my personal recommendation is the Pepper Steak.
Weekday lunch buffet 11:30 a.m. - 2:30 p.m. Open Mon. - Fri. 11 a.m. - 10 p.m., Sat. 11 a.m. - 12 a.m., Sun. 12 p.m. - 9 p.m.

2 of the Best Pizza Joints Around

Aurelio's and Enrico's win my vote for "best pizza" in the South Suburbs. They leave Gino's, Lou Malnatti's, and Leona's eating their dust, or should I say crust.

Aurelio's Pizza
23 Oak Street
815/469-2196
Aurelio's is a down-to-earth, family restaurant located in the heart of downtown Frankfort. If we were playing the word association game and you said Aurelio's, I'd say cheese fries, combination basket, cheese pizza, and spinach Calabrese. These are only a few of the mouth-watering selections that have made the Aurelio's name synonymous with excellence.

The combination of crispy crust, spices, sweet sauce, and the perfect amount of cheese makes their pizza stand above others. Other items on the menu are appetizers (combination basket, cheese fries, fried zucchini, and pizza bread); sandwiches (meatball, Italian beef, sausage, submarine, and burgers); pasta (ravioli, mostaccioli, and spaghetti); salads; and desserts. Being a sandwich maker at Aurelio's was my first job, and I made it my duty to eat everything on the menu because I knew one day I'd have to review the place for you. Though all dishes win "thumbs up," repeat after me: cheese pizza, combination basket, cheese fries, and spinach Calabrese.
Other locations in Homewood, Joliet, and New Lenox. Open Mon. - Sat. 11 a.m. - 10 p.m., Sun. 3 p.m. - 10 p.m.

Enrico's
427 N. LaGrange Rd.
815/469-4187
Enrico's casual family restaurant offers a thicker, spicier pizza consisting of a bubbly crust topped with huge portions of cheese, sausage, and other goodies. After sampling the pizza, branch out to the beef sandwich on garlic bread, California pizza salad (weedy greens and veggies on a pita), huge nachos with all the fun stuff,

and French onion soup with jumbo croutons and lots of gooey cheese on top.
Open Mon. - Fri. 4:30 p.m. - 10 p.m., Sat. - Sun. 4 p.m. - 11:30 p.m.

Rising Sun
442 LaGrange Rd.
815/469-6688
Rising Sun's carry out menu includes the basics of Cantonese and Mandarin cuisine. Take note of the excellent sweet and sour chicken—huge chunks of fried chicken, sauce, and freshly-cut pineapples, tomatoes, and peppers over rice.
Open Tues. - Thurs. 11 a.m - 10 p.m., Fri. - Sat. 11 a.m. - 11 p.m., Sun. 11a.m. - 9 p.m.

Mary Todd's
Frankfort Town Center
695 LaGrange Rd.
815/469-9122
Local yokels know that Mary Todd's cafe started off in a little building on the outskirts of town and blossomed into one of the hottest restaurants around. When they moved into a larger space, Mary Todd's added an improved antique, 1860s decor more suitable for the quality of the food, which enhances the entire dining experience. The menu offers appetizers like red fried tomatoes or salads like the Mary's Salad, a bed of lettuce topped with tortellini, shrimp, chicken, and assorted vegetables. A sandwich highlight is the North and South (corned beef, roast beef, Swiss, and American on marble rye), while chicken stir fry is a dinner favorite. Mary Todd's beautiful new dining facilities include a separate ice cream parlor and a bar.
Appetizers $1.50-$5.95, salads $6.25-$7.25, sandwiches $4.95-$6.95, entrees $8.25-$11.95. Restaurant open daily 6 a.m. - 10 p.m.

Best Sports Bar in Frankfort

Chef Klaus Steak and Seafood (Owned by Die Bier Stube)
Frankfort Town Center
695 LaGrange Rd.
815/469-0940
Yes, a cool bar in Frankfort! And its name is Chef Klaus Steak and Seafood. I know, it's not your typical "cool bar" name, but the other half is a restaurant for the fine diners who enjoy steak and lobster ($12-$18)—just ignore them. Unless, of course, you like feasting

on steak, lobster, seafood, gourmet cheeses, and desserts while listening to a live pianist. If you prefer fries, sandwiches, salads, and appetizers ($5-$10), you're better off hanging out in the bar area playing darts.
Open daily 11 a.m. - 10 p.m.

Best Homemade Bowl

Cactus Carols
116 Kansas Street
815/469-4448
As kids growing up in Frankfort, we all knew who Carol Watson, a.k.a. Cactus Carol, was: the woman who wore big hats and frequented garage sales. Items and collectibles from those same garage sales now decorate her famous restaurant, Cactus Carols. This is a great place to go on a first date or if you're dating a dud who can't start a conversation to save his/her life. The knick-knacks, antiques, different tables with unmatching chairs, bar, books, and other items will spark conversation bound to outlast dinner. Who knows? You may be able to ID items from your past garage sales. The restaurant serves a killer cheese soup in a homemade bread bowl.
Open Thurs. - Fri. 5:30 p.m. - 9 p.m., Sat 5:30 p.m. - 10 p.m.

Best Meat Meet Market

Ambrosino's Italian Market and Deli
Vineyard Plaza
50495 S. La Grange Rd.
815/464-5002
What a great place to stop at on the way home from work for homemade pastas, ravioli, hams, subs, salads, sausages, olive oils, pasta sauces, breads, imported cheeses, meats, and attractive men. What? I don't want readers out there to get the wrong idea, but being a single female I tend to notice when there is a large quantity of quality single males in a given area, what I call the "malequalyquan factor." Therefore, it's my duty to inform you that every time I go into this deli it's full of good-looking young businessmen, firemen, policemen, etc. I'm not recommending hanging out here all day with a log of sausage and a chunk of provolone, but it is a great place to pop in and pick up dinner or lunch.
Open Mon. - Fri. 9 a.m. - 7 p.m., Sat. 9 a.m. - 6 p.m., Sun. 9 a.m. - 2 p.m.

Turtles, Blizzards, and Extraterrestrials, Oh My!

The Creamery
459 W. Nebraska
815/469-2107
Open only during the ice cream eating months, this little wooden building on the corner of Rt. 45 and Nebraska put Frankfort on the sweet-tooth map. On an average day, the parking lot is full, the two lines extend far into the parking lot, and cars line the streets. Are they giving away gold, money, time-share vacations? Better, they make sundaes, slushes, malts, and other specialty desserts that obviously keep people coming back.
Call for hours.

Courtyard Bistro
21 White Street
815/464-1404
You will be pleased to know this posh new bistro (hidden off Center Road by the Trolley Barn) offers the entire fine dining package: exquisite food, a great atmosphere, and top-notch service. High-back, Abe Lincoln chairs and fine crystal on the white, linen-clad tables create an antiquated 1860s look, which contrasts nicely with the modern marble bar area.

The menu lists appetizers on the order of smoked salmon capriccio, baked onion leek tart, and grilled vegetable goat cheese purse, while Jamaican jerk chicken, whiskey herb marinated rack of pork, and butternut squash ravioli are among the entree choices. Desserts include creme brulee and New Orleans Bread Pudding.
Appetizers $3-$8; most entrees $14-$16; most desserts, soups, and salads $3-$4. Open for lunch Tues. - Sat. 11 a.m. - 3 p.m., for dinner Tues. - Thurs. 4 p.m. - 10 p.m., Fri. - Sat. 4 p.m. - 11 p.m., Sun. 4 p.m. - 9 p.m.

Chicago Sun-Times Rated One of the Best

Rosie's Diner
340 N. LaGrange Rd.
815/469-7160
The *Chicago Sun-Times* rated Rosie's gyros as one of the best in the Chicagoland area. Besides five different gyros specialties, they have nine types of burgers, eight hot dog varieties, hoagies, super

sausages, sandwiches such as rib eye, and hot and spicy chicken.

While all the diner's items are commendable, we suggest the double cheeseburger with grilled onions, the Gyros combo, or the bag of fries, which gives new meaning to the phrase "large fries"—it's a literal heap!
Sandwiches $.90 - $4.99. Open Sun. - Mon. 11 a.m. - 8 p.m., Tues. - Sat. 11 a.m. - 9 p.m.

SHOPPING

The General Store
119 Kansas Street
815/469-4002
Residents of Frankfort, especially those with a sweet tooth, know this establishment well. It was *the* place to go for old-fashioned candy and sweets, especially rock candy. If only to experience the atmosphere of an 1800s general store and admire the building, you too should visit when in town: built in 1870, the building served as the town's general store even then. Besides sweets, the store is packed from top to bottom with replicas of advertising signs, kitchen ware, cookie cutters, holiday decorations, soap, candles, crafts, food mixes, jams, jellies, honey, Amish candy, pasta, syrup, and more.
Open Mon. - Sat. 10 a.m. - 4:30 p.m., Sun. 12 p.m. - 5 p.m.

Twice Voted the Southland's #1 Place to Buy Antiques

Antiques Unique
100 Kansas St.
815/469-2741
An Underpriced Antique Dealer? Is there such a thing? Well, Antiques Unique is close enough. Co-owner Shirley Walsh believes in passing along a good deal. Housed in an 1866 building and former post office, this shops is a good place for lovers of antique saucers and cups, English collectibles, and beveled and stained glass. Other specialties are clocks, amber, and Celtic jewelry. Shirley is also a good resource person, and if she doesn't have something, she may be able to hook you up with someone who does.
Open Tues. - Sat 10 a.m. - 5 p.m., Sun. 10 a.m. - 5 p.m. Closed Mon.

Black Smith Shops
12 N. Smith St.
c. 1870

Black Smith Shops include:

For those Sick People Who Christmas Shop Year Round...

Mitchell's Frankfort Christmas Corner
815/469-2444
I'm not saying the owners of Frankfort Christmas Corner are demented, but they have dedicated their store to Christmas. Yuletide items include Christopher Radko: Rising Star, Possible Dreams Santa, Snowbabies-Dept 56, Charming Tails, personalized ornaments, limited edition collectibles, sports ornaments, and more. Believe it or not, this is the only year-round Christmas shop in the Southwest Suburbs.
Open Mon. - Sat. 10 a.m. - 5 p.m., Sun. 12 p.m. - 5 p.m.

Great Place to Find Newer Children's Toys

Price is Right Resale Shop
815/464-1886
Some items you'll find "priced right" include children's, women's, and men's clothing; books (I've found a 1918 leather-bound book in very good condition here for 50 cents); clocks; pictures; cameras; jewelry; figurines; advertising memorabilia; and furniture. This is a great place to find popular children's toy's still in great shape—things like Fisher Price toy sets complete with animals and people, Cabbage Patch dolls, complete games, and stuffed animals.
Open Tues. & Fri. 10 a.m. - 4 p.m., Wed. & Thurs. 10 a.m. - 5 p.m., Sat. 10 a.m. - 5 p.m., Sun. 12 p.m. - 4 p.m.

Hidden Gem

All Small
815/469-4111
All Small is a haven for doll houses, doll furniture, other miniatures, and appropriate building supplies. Some of these small scale items are imported from Europe, while some are made especially for the store by a local artist. They carry hundreds of bedrooms sets, chandeliers, knick-knacks, tables, and dining room sets, from all eras from the 1700s to the present. The detail and intricate designs

of the dolls, dresses, fire places, stained glass, and furniture are stunning.
Open Mon. - Sat. 10 a.m. - 5 p.m., Sun. 12 p.m. - 5 p.m.

Best Deals You Keep Driving By

Crafty Cow
(In a restored house directly after **Alsip Home & Nursery**, see p. 5.)
20555 S. La Grange Rd.
815/464-7088
Crafty Cow is the kind of store you constantly drive by and think, "gee, I wonder what's in there," but never bother to stop and look. The bi-level store is divided into sections that are leased by consignors who then sell their own items. Each space blends nicely with the next, so it doesn't look like a confusing mess, like most stores that practice this method. Merchants deal predominantly in crafty items: bears, wood crafts, holiday goods, ornaments, wooden figure Santas, wreaths, furniture, rag dolls, baskets and basket garters, candles, home made mixes for muffins and cakes, Victorian cards and prints. Prices are surprisingly low for the detail and quality of the items.
Open Tues. - Sat. 10 a.m. - 5 p.m., Sun. 11 a.m. - 4 p.m.

Smallest Store One Can Get Lost In

Amazing Fantasy Books & Comics
47 E. Lincoln Hwy.
815/469-5092
http://www.nlenx.com/mack/afbooks
Common to the vocabulary of patrons is "crap," as in, "Crap, look what time it is! I've been in here for hours!" Racks holding all the latest comic books and reference guides adorn the walls and the newest and most popular action figures, figurines, and collectibles flaunt themselves by the check-out counter. Bookshelves overflow with classic literature, new age material, collectible price books, and self-published comics. For insert and collectible cards, as well as hard-to-find, rare comics such as Captain Marvel, Fantastic Four, and other classics, there is counter service. To protect and preserve all your purchases, comic and card protectors are available.
Also located in Tinley Park, Lockport, and Calumet City. Open Mon: - Thurs. 11 a.m. - 8 p.m., Fri. 11 a.m. - 12 a.m., Sat. 11 a.m. - 7 p.m., Sun. 11 a.m. - 5 p.m.

Voted "Best of Chicago's Southland" for Interior Designs

The Great Room
Lincoln Hwy 1/2 mile east of LaGrange Rd.
Unincorporated Frankfort
815/464-6446
One of the South Suburbs' newest and most welcomed additions, The Great Room was sent from the houseware gods to solve this problem. Those of us living in the South Suburbs have all felt the pains of searching for housewares, decorations, or a piece of furniture that weren't available anywhere but up north—in The City. Customers come from as far as Naperville, Downers Grove, and Indiana to see what's for sale.
Open Mon. 11 a.m. - 7 p.m., Tues. - Sat. 10 a.m. - 5 p.m., Sun. 12 p.m. - 4 p.m.

Brides in the Attic
20555 LaGrange Rd.
815/464-6030
Top five ways to get your money's worth from an expensive bridesmaid dress/bridal gown after you've worn it: 1) Volunteer to chaperone every prom in a 50-mile radius for the next 20 years. 2) Place an ad in the paper so that strange people can come over to try it on, rip it, get deodorant on it, and then not buy it. 3) Trying to break up with your boyfriend? Nothing says "I've got issues" like wearing a bridesmaid dress to the bowling alley. 4) The next time your church is holding auditions for *Carrie*, campaign hard for the lead. Then use the dress for the prom scene and write the cost off on your tax return. 5) Take it to Brides in the Attic, a wedding consignment store that sells "gently worn" dresses as well as vintage dresses.
Open Mon., Wed., & Thurs. 11 a.m. - 8 p.m., Fri. 11 a.m. - 7 p.m., Sat. 10 a.m. - 5 p.m., Sun. 12 p.m. - 4 p.m.

Candle Cottage
18 W. Elwood
815/469-9773
Vanilla, cherry, blah blah blah. Everyone likes a candle store with original scents like pecan, pomegranate, and peppermint. Candle Cottage not only makes such appetizing scents, but candle designs and molds as well. In fact, they'll customize candles for you with any color/scent combination you like. Defy candle norms by ordering

a green candle that smells like vanilla or a red candle redolent of blueberries. Check back often for sales on their homemade candles.
Open Mon. - Fri. 10 a.m. - 6 p.m., Sat. 10 a.m. - 5 p.m., Sun. 11 a.m. - 4 p.m.

Barn With The Most Hidden Treasures

Trolley Barn
11 S. White St.
815/464-1060
Trolley Barn is an antique marketplace in a rehabbed turn-of-the-century barn that houses over 45 dealers. Unless you forget your wallet at home, it's almost impossible not to buy something at one of these stores.
Open Mon. - Fri. 10 a.m. - 8 p.m., Sat. 10 a.m. - 6 p.m., Sun. 12 p.m. - 6 p.m.

Stores in the Trolley Barn:

White Street Gallery & Framing
815/469-1216
Definitely worth a visit, White Street Gallery displays breathtaking country prints as well as impressionist and abstract works, including original paintings and limited edition prints from nationally known artists as well as popular Frankfort area artists, such as Sam Hageman, Steven Lotysz, R.R. Benda, and many more.

Wicked Yet Relaxing

Terra Firma
815/469-9324
This interesting store sells aromatherapy candles, oils and incense, along with metaphysical stones, tarot cards, dream guides, and spell and herb books. A bead bar in the back of the store is used by those who prefer to make their own jewelry.
Also located in Homewood.

Treat Street
815/464-4466
Besides making sundaes, shakes, and malts, Treat Street sells Long Grove Candles, popcorn, soft pretzels, Jelly Belly jellybeans, country fresh fudge, and old-fashioned candies. My personal favorite is the

fat free chocolate brownie ice cream. I verified several times that it was actually fat free, since the rich taste and large chunks of cocoa and fudge made me wonder.

Ass-Kicking Spice Store

Fire & Spice
815/464-1005
The rows and rows of hot sauces, spices from around the world, salsas, gourmet food items, olive oils, chili mixes, cookbooks, glassware, gift items, customized or premade gift baskets, pastas, microbrews, and wines kick butt. I've tried a couple of the hotter sauces and I am here to say that labels reading "hot as hell", "ass kicking", and "last rites" all carry valid descriptions. They frequently offer samples—proceed with caution.

The Fisherman's Wife
815/464-6480
Are you suffering from Amish-built furniture withdrawal? Then I suggest you pay a visit to The Fisherman's Wife before visiting the larger furniture stores. You may find a very unique piece for less than if you went to Darwin or Ethan Allen. I like their cabinets and the bookshelf that is really a canoe sliced in half.

Geri Ann's
815/464-4438
Have a pretty lamp with a gaudy shade? Geri Ann's specialty is lampshade design and consultation. Not just a cute store with better quality merchandise, they stock a few items not seen elsewhere. Also for sale are higher quality decorations, ornaments, pictures and prints, Victorian picture frames and furniture, unique lithoplane night-lights and lamps, and other miscellaneous items of the same ilk.

Storehouse of Knowledge
815/464-1060
How many times have you wanted to walk into a store and order some knowledge? While there may not be hope for you, there may still be hope for your children. Storehouse of Knowledge is a learning shop dedicated to family values, culture, creativity, and education.

Gold 'N' Chains
815/469-1747
Gold 'N' Chains offers a large selection of fine jewelry, 14K gold, sterling silver, and gemstones. (A repair service is also available.) They also carry brand name purses, watches, and colognes at wholesale prices.

New To You Children's Resale Shop
Butter Plaza
629 LaGrange Rd.
815/464-0084
New To You sells infant to pre-teen clothing, furniture, toys, collectible dolls, bedding, and many other items. Unless your infant highly uses Mega-Memory, I highly doubt that he/she will remember—or care—that they are wearing second-hand clothes. This is the perfect store for parents who want to save money without sacrificing name brand fashion. They are taking consignors.

Discount Records
Rt. 30 and Rt. 45 (next to Jewel)
815/464-5444
Discount Records is a primary source for music in the Frankfort area. They have excellent prices on CDs, cassettes, and rock memorabilia. If you're ready to part with your Spice Girls or Yanni CD, this is also a great place to sell CDs as they pay a slightly higher price than most places.
Open Mon. - Sat. 10 a.m. - 9 p.m., Sun. 11 a.m. - 5 p.m.

LODGING

The Abe Lincoln Motel
Rt. 30 between Frankfort and Mokena
815/469-5114
It's time to debunk a local myth. During my search I could not prove that Abe Lincoln once stayed in this small, one-level motel with 12 rooms and modern facilities. Another published misconception is that the bricks were molded by hand out of mud and grass. That would've been cool, but it's not true. Note: this motel is of the flea bag variety, lodge at your own risk.

SPECIAL EVENTS

Frankfort Annual Car Show and Swap
Downtown Frankfort
708/532-4606
(Tom DeJan of the Frankfort Car Club)
On the last Sunday in July, weather permitting, the Frankfort Car Club hosts its annual Car Show and Swap in downtown Frankfort, which is closed off to make way for about 300-400 cars in approximately 20 different classes. 50-100 flea market vendors sell everything from car models to polish. In total, some 5,000 people come to see the polished metal and witness the judging and awarding of trophies.
Admission is free for viewers. Pre-registered cars are charged $10/car, otherwise it's $15/car.

Driving Tips

Avoid Rt. 45 and Rt. 30 on the weekends and during rush hour. Some alternate routes include Wolf and Laraway Roads.

Cruisin' Night
Did you miss the car show? Then you must go to the Trolley Barn on Thursdays from 6 p.m. to 10 p.m., weather permitting, where all the admirers and owners of antique and special-interest cars will be strutting their stuff. Just remember: no drag racing. The speed limit is 25 m.p.h. in those parts.

Largest Craft Fest in the Midwest

Frankfort Fall Festival
Downtown Frankfort
Labor Day weekend
If you haven't heard of the famous Frankfort Fall Fest, you must be living under a rock. During Labor Day weekend the entire downtown area is blocked off from traffic and hundreds of vendors line the streets. Over 250,000 people from all over the country travel to Frankfort to buy antiques and crafts, eat food (the aroma of grilled corn on the cob is inescapable), listen to live music, relax in the beer tent, and hang out at the carnival.

Annual Harvest Fest and Native American Indian Event
Late September
Breidert's Green in downtown Frankfort
815/469-3356
Admission is free.

Frankfort Regulations:
Fleshlings and the Flow of Sewers

"Solid or viscous substances in quantities or of such size capable of causing obstruction to the flow of sewers such, but not limited to, ashes, cinders, sand, mud, straw, shavings, metal, glass, rags, feathers, tar, plastics, wood, underground garbage, whole blood, paunch manure, hair and fleshlings, entrails and paper dishes, cups, milk containers and the like, either whole or ground by garbage grinders."

If someone dumps enough "fleshling, hair and whole blood" to clog a sewer, stop worrying about ordinances and start calling the police!

GLENWOOD

Just The Facts

Village of Glenwood
Home of the First Black Cemetery in Illinois
20 miles south of Chicago

Median Age	36.3
Median Family Income	$49,298
Average Sale Price of Home	$107,691

Population:

1990	9,289
1994	9,249
2010	8,855

Contacts:
Village Hall 708/758-5150
http://www.lincolnnet.net/communities/glenwood/glenwood.htm

Access via:
I-80/294

HISTORY

Though land purchases in the area had occurred as early as 1838, the first settlers didn't arrive in Glenwood until 1846. In 1871, due to the region's number of wooded glens, the town's name was changed from Hickory Bend to Glenwood. Today Glenwood remains a quiet village surrounded by farms and forest preserves.

We're #1! We're #1!

Thomas Borrows, a farmer and stock raiser, was an employee of the Galena Railroad. He hauled the first ties for the Rock Island line into Chicago.

Mount Glenwood Cemetery
18301 Glenwood-Thornton Rd.
708/758-5663
Established around the 1890s, Mount Glenwood was the first cemetery in the Chicago area to desegregate, and today is recognized as the first black cemetery in Illinois. In the early 1900s, African Americans who died in Chicago and surrounding areas were transported on the Illinois Central train from La Salle and Clark to the cemetery. The founder of the Black Muslims and the Nation of Islam, Elijah Muhammad, is buried here, as well as Fred Slater, the first African American circuit court judge in Illinois; Charles Gavin, the first African American orthopedic surgeon; and Major Taylor, the first African American Olympic gold medalist in biking.

TOURING

Glenwood School For Boys
c. 1887
Glenwood is one of the finest private, not-for-profit, educational communities for boys from disadvantaged families in the country. Glenwood School for Boys has two campuses: the South Campus, which is located on 172 acres in the Village of Glenwood, and the West Campus, which is located on 120 acres in unincorporated St. Charles.

Who's Who

The Kansas City Chief's tight end, Derrick Walker, was born in Glenwood.

The school was founded by Oscar Dudley with the help of other men, including Robert Todd Lincoln, the son of Abraham Lincoln.

ENTERTAINMENT

Country Club Paintball
537 W. 159th
708/756-1166
CCP maintains a 31,000-square-foot indoor paintball arena. Paintballs cost $.05 - $.08 per pellet based on quantity. You must be at least ten years of age to participate in this messy sport.
Deposit required for all reservations. Open Thurs. 5 p.m. - 10 p.m., Fri. 5 p.m. - 12 a.m., Sat. 12 p.m. - 12 a.m., Sun. 12 p.m. - 9 p.m.

FOOD

Best Place to Have Breakfast

Gabe's Place
9 East Main St.
708/757-7171
Gabe's Place attracts crowds from all surrounding towns. On any given Sunday the place is packed from the early a.m. hours until well after lunch. However, the wait rarely exceeds 20 minutes since the service is quick and seating, with well over 20 tables, is abundant.

Though service is speedy, Gabe's doesn't skimp in the kitchen. The blueberry pancakes are actually "real" blueberry pancakes loaded with berries, not just plain pancakes topped with blueberry syrup. Vegetables are grilled before they're put into omelettes for a much better taste. (Double thumbs and fingers up for the omelettes!) Other winning menu items include Gabe's Omelette (feta cheese, tomato, and onions); an Italian sausage omelette; pecan, blueberry, or chocolate chip pancakes; and the pancake sandwich. Among their many sandwiches and burgers is the highly recommend blue cheeseburger. Friday evenings are all-you-can-eat-nights (choose from fried chicken, perch, Alaskan whitefish, and shrimp); prices start at $6 and include soup, cole slaw, salad, biscuits, and dessert.
Breakfast items $3.75-$5.10. Open Sat. - Thurs. 6 a.m. - 3 p.m., Fri. 6 a.m. - 9 p.m.

SHOPPING

Annie Lee & Friends Art Gallery
37 E. Main St.
708/757-7100
This gallery features original art by nationally known artist Annie Lee and a gift shop with neat gifts and hundreds of collectibles.
Open Mon. - Sat. 11 a.m. - 7 p.m.

Trivia

Glenwood was reportedly a stop on the Chicago-Vincennes Pony Express Route.

HARVEY

Just The Facts

City of Harvey
"Hub of the South Suburbs"

Contact:
Village Hall 708/339-4200

Access via:
I-294, I-80, and Rt. 1 and 83

FOOD

Gino's Steak House
16299 Wallace Ave.
708/331-4393
Gino's was voted as one of the top ten steakhouses in the U.S. by the *Chicago Tribune* and the best steakhouse in the Southland by *Star Publications.*
Open Sun. & Tues.- Thurs. 11 a.m. - 9 p.m., Mon. 11 a.m. - 11 p.m., Fri. 11 a.m. - 12 a.m., Sat. 12 p.m. - 12 a.m.

Trivia

Harvey is the third largest employment center in the Chicago Southland.

Famous Who's Who of Harvey

Seven-time all star Lou Boudreau (1917-) played for the Cleveland Indians right out of high school. By the age of 24 he became baseball's youngest manager/player. Six years later he led the team to its first World Championship since 1920 while earning himself MVP honors. Today he is considered to be the best shortstop in Cleveland Indian history. His amazing career ended in 1952 after a stint with the Red Sox, and he was inducted into the Hall of Fame in 1970.

Gilbert Ames Bliss (1876-1951) was a brilliant mathematician and educator known mostly for his calculus variations. He was the department chairman from 1927-1941 at the University of Chicago.

Born in Harvey and educated at Northwestern University, the University of Illinois, and the School of the Art Institute of Chicago, the gifted American painter Ivan Albright (1897-1983) concentrated on capturing corruption and the darker side of things on his canvases. Some of his paintings include "God Created Man In His Own Image", "That Which I Should Have Done I Did Not Do", "Portrait of Mary Block", and "The Picture of Dorian Gray." The latter three are part of the collection of the Art Institute of Chicago.

Blues/jazz pianist Arthur Hodes (1904-1993) performed with Bix Beiderbecke, Gene Krupa, Eddie Condon, and Wild Bill Davison before leaving Chicago in 1938 for New York City. There he hosted a jazz radio program on WNYC; published, wrote, and edited his own monthly magazine, the *Jazz Record*; performed with the bands of Jose Marsala and Mezz Mezzrow; and recorded piano solos with his own short-lived record company.

Also hailing from Harvey was Ira Murchison (1933-1994), U.S. gold medal winner for the 4-100-meter relay in the 1956 Melbourne, Australia games. Not only did Ira win the gold, but he did it in a world-record time of 39.5 seconds. That year he also held the world record for the 100-meter at 10.2 seconds.

HOMEWOOD

Just The Facts

Village of Homewood
"Village of Friendly Living"
25 miles south of Chicago

Land Area	5.30 sq. miles
Median Age	38.1
Median Family Income	$53,605
Average Sale Price of Home	$129,311

Population:

1990	19,278
1994	20,061
2010	20,120

Contact:
Village Hall 708/798-3000

Access via:
Interstate highways I-80, I-94, I-294, and I-57, Rt. 1, Volmer Rd., and Western Ave.

HISTORY

Since the 1830s pioneers from Europe had traveled to Homewood via the Vincennes Trail, but it wasn't until 1853 that James Hart settled in the area and named it Hartford. As with so many nearby towns, the name soon changed (to Thornton Station) to match the name of the Illinois Central Railroad stop there. When the area was incorporated in 1893, it took the new name of Homewood.

After Homewood's incorporation, the Illinois Central Railroad shuttled golfers from Chicago who had discovered Homewood's plush courses and green country clubs. Some enjoyed the area so much they started building their summer homes here.

Homewood is a mature, quaint, peaceful town and has become one of Chicago Southland's most enjoyable centers for a day of shopping. The downtown area provides a picturesque backdrop with red brick walkways, old-fashioned benches on the street corners, 1900s-style black street lamps, and plush trees. Dozens of restaurants, resale shops, boutiques, cafes, specialty stores, and parks exist in the walking area, and plenty of street parking is available.

TOURING

The **Homewood-Flossmoor Park District** (3301 Flossmoor Rd., 708/957-0300), one of the best in the state, offers thirty parks, a racquet and fitness club, an ice arena, and a large community center.

Richard D. Irwin Park
Ridge Road across from The Village Door (see below)
This large park has a circle walkway interrupted every so often by benches and lampposts. A picnic table, gazebo, and playground extend beyond the circle surrounding a sculpture by Margot McMahon entitled "Formation of a Lasting Relationship: Father and Child."
Open dawn - dusk.

Village Door Dry Cleaners
1940 Ridge Rd.
708/799-2266
Village Door Dry Cleaners has transformed its front lobby into a "museum." The large, wooden and glass display cases were crafted in 1869 and contain antique sewing items, salesmen's sewing machine samples, Singer ads, political buttons, daguerreotypes, and more. Upon a shelf behind the counter sits a huge Victrola that would make any 78-RPM collector drool. You'll be happy to know that the equipment used to wash and dry clean clothes is not one of these antiques. Be sure to pop in and take a look.
Open Mon. - Fri. 7 a.m. - 6:30 p.m., Sat. 7 a.m. - 5:30 p.m. Closed Sun.

FOOD

Balagio
18042 Martin Ave.
708/957-1650
The moment you enter Balagio you'll be swept away by the beauty and romance of Italy. Well, it's not really Italy (I hope you knew that), but the decorators did a great job of bringing that atmosphere to this spacious restaurant through its murals, old-fashioned lamps, and climbing vines.

Some of their delicious dinners include the veal rib chop, ricotta manicotti, cavatelli, penne with eggplant, Fettuccine Alfredo, and cheese ravioli. There's more! Balagio also serves veal piccata, roasted chicken with wine and garlic sauce, pork chops, and ribs with oregano, olive oil and garlic.

When the meal is over and the server asks how it was, answer, "[The] cibo fu eccellente. Mio complimenti al chef. Oh, giê, I'll possesso quello libero bottiglia di vino presente." That loosely translates to "The food was excellent. My compliments to the chef. Oh, yeah, I'll take that free bottle of wine now."
Entrees $8.95-$17.95. Open Mon. - Sat. for lunch 11 a.m. - 3 p.m., for dinner Mon. - Thurs. 5 p.m. - 10 p.m., Fri . -Sat. 5 p.m. - 11 p.m.

Bogart's Charhouse
8225 Dixie Highway
708/798-2000
See the description under *Tinley Park*, p. 208.
Open for lunch Mon. - Fri. 11 a.m. - 4 p.m., for dinner Mon. - Thurs. 4 p.m. - 10 p.m., Fri. 4 p.m. - 11 p.m., Sat. 12 p.m. - 11 p.m., Sun. 12 p.m. - 9 p.m.

The Southland's Oldest Restaurant

Surma's Restaurant
17501 Dixie Hwy.
708/798-0327
Surma's menu consists of prime rib, seafood, and fried chicken so good it's been voted "Best Fried Chicken in the Southland" two years in a row.
Open Sun. & Tues. - Wed. 11 a.m. - 9 p.m.; Mon., Thurs., & Sat. 11 a.m. - 9 p.m., Fri. 11 a.m. - 10 p.m.

Bears and Wildcats Eat Their BBQ Sauce

The Washington Square Restaurant
17815 S. Halsted St.
708/957-8881
The Washington Square Restaurant offers a friendly, family-style dining environment with a varied menu. Breakfasts start around $3 and include double-yolk eggs, crepes, waffles, omelettes, and skillet meals. Lunches and dinners at about $5 include fried chicken, fajitas, and gyros. The house specialty is the BBQ, baby back ribs, which I highly recommend ordering up smoked and smothered in what is some of the best BBQ sauce around. No wonder it is the official sauce of the Chicago Bears and Northwestern Wildcats.
Open daily 6 a.m. - 11 p.m.

"The Townie Restaurant and Hang Out"

Tom's Family Restaurant
944 Ridge Road
708/798-1311
This dominantly pink restaurant is one of the friendliest we've had the pleasure of dining at. It's a popular meeting spot for locals and even has a play area for children in the front. Dinners include prime rib, perch, orange roughy, pork chops, and steaks, while gyros,

Ruebens, and Rachels are among the tastier sandwiches.
Dinners $5-$8.80, sandwiches $2.45-$5.20. Open daily 6 a.m. - 11 p.m. daily.

The Busiest Kitchen in Homewood

Dave's Kitchen
2044 Ridge Rd.
708/922-0993
What a hopping—and homey—place! Carol, a server, wins the award for being able to sustain the most stress without flipping out. She can cater to a packed restaurant of four large tables, five booths, and 12 bar seats and still have time to make the visit enjoyable for each customer. She'll strike up a conversation as if she's known you for years.

Dave's unique menu offers his Beast, original chili (delivers a zingy kick), six-way grilled cheese, and homemade chips. The Beast involves a huge pile of four eggs—cooked with enough chopped ham to reconstruct a pig, Colby cheese, and peppers served on a French roll with garlic butter. Hands down the biggest sandwich we've seen on the book-writing journey.

The six-way grilled cheese consists of three slices of wheat bread layered with American, Swiss, mozzarella, Colby, and Jack cheeses and sprinkled with Parmesan. This fine dairy blend evokes that "I'm stuffed like a pig, but I gotta have another bite" feeling. Speaking of cheese, a majority of orders coming out of the kitchen are cheeseburger variations and Philly steak sandwiches.

Salads, taco burgers, turkey burgers, hot dogs, and miscellaneous sandwiches complete the food choices at this fast paced and entertaining family eatery.
Most menu items $2-$5. Open Mon. - Fri. 11 a.m. - 7: 30 p.m., Sat. - Sun. 8 a.m. - 2 p.m.

SHOPPING

If You Want To Have the Coolest Gift At the Baby Shower...

Bella Luna
Corner of Dixie Hwy. and Ridge Rd.
708/798-3410
For original gift ideas, stop by Bella Luna as an alternative to hitting the mall. While a section dedicated to women's fashion has tempting goods like a basic black dress with brocade flowers with a jacket to match ($175), the highlight of the store is the baby section. Here you'll find clothing—from adorable flowered hats ($14) to unique outfits ($21); hand-painted furniture like a rocker ($85) with a matching toy chest; and accessories such as bottles, picture frames, and stuffed animals.
Open Mon. - Wed., Fri. 9 a.m. - 5:30 p.m., Thurs. 9:30 a.m. - 8 p.m., Sat. 10 a.m. - 5 p.m.

Fish That Can Swallow You Whole

Natalie Interiors and Gallery
2009 Ridge Rd.
708/647-1177
Looking for something different to decorate your home? This gallery of distinctive housewares and gift items exhibits one-of-a-kind art, the Edna Hibel collection, fairy tale dolls, hand-painted country art, hand-painted large wooden mirrors with matching dressers, brand

A trompe l'oeil painting in Homewood's downtown shopping district.

new reproductions of antiques, a variety of golf and fishing crafts, art deco inspired gifts, Coca-Cola collectibles, large water color paintings of famous golf courses, painted tiles, Eglomise, colorful pottery, rugs, bottles, and more. The prize winner for most unusual item seen on our South Suburban shopping spree? Huge, watercolor fish sculptures to hang on the wall.
Open Mon. - Wed. & Fri - Sat. 10 a.m. - 5 p.m., Thurs. 10 a.m. - 8 p.m. Closed Sun.

Calling All Bibliophiles

Autumn Leaves Books, Inc.
18029 S. Dixie Hwy.
708/922-3522
Located on one of Homewood's main drags, this medium-sized bookstore carries new, used, and collectible books. Tall shelving units hold books from the 1800s to the present and include entire sets of such authors as Dickens and Wells. Ephemera and vintage advertisements paper the walls and offer other scenery to peruse besides the books. Any avid book collector will tell you that their prices are a steal!
Open Mon. - Sat. 10 a.m. - 7 p.m.

Blackberry Harvest Dollhouse Museum Shoppe
18120 Dixie Highway
708/957-4332
A must for any doll collector and a store you won't find anywhere else! Blackberry Harvest opened in October of 1997 and has since been home to an unbelievable selection of dollhouses and accessories.
Open Wed., Fri., & Sat. 10 a.m. - 6 p.m., Thurs. 12:30 p.m. - 8 p.m.

Duo's Nearly Nu Resale Shop
2015 Ridge Rd.
708/798-0075
This store carries designer fashions for women no more than two years old and in excellent condition. Furs (Carson Pirie Scott - $350), business suits and skirts (Henry Bendel - $150), shoes (some never worn), jewelry (vintage and new), purses (newer fashionable and antique cocktail), hats, belts, scarves, and more fill the racks. By the front door sat an oriental dining set and china cabinet for sale. An antique china set (c. late 1800s) was stunning and is selling

for $350.
Open Mon. - Wed. & Fri. 10 a.m. - 6 p.m., Thurs. 10 a.m. - 7 p.m., Sat. 10 a.m. - 5 p.m.

The Village Door
18100 Martin Ave.
708/798-8665
This large consignment store is filled with quality furniture, rugs, jewelry, linens, silverware, artwork, china, milk glass, platters and plates, lamps, picture frames, Depression glass, vintage toys, books, brass, and more. All proceeds go to the Cancer Support Center.
Open Mon. 10 a.m. - 2 p.m. (for incoming consignments only), Tues. - Sat. 10 a.m. - 5 p.m.

Terra Firma
2048 Ridge Rd.
708/799-2265
This store is a little larger than the Frankfort location (see p. 66) and stocks more brocade hats, purses, Beanie Babies, and craft items than the other shop.

LODGING

Best Western
17400 S. Halsted St.
708/957-1600
This Best Western has a 202-room capacity, plus an indoor/outdoor pool, banquet facilities, bridal suites, childcare, complimentary continental breakfast, and restaurant. Rooms are equipped with air conditioning, coffee maker, color TV with cable, hair dryer, and king-size bed.

JOLIET

Just The Facts

City of Joliet
"City of Champions"
"Prison town"
40 miles southwest of Chicago

Land Area	34.6 sq. miles
Median Age	28.8
Median Household Income	$42,000
Average Sale Price of Home	$98,612

Contacts:
City Hall 815/724-4000
http://www.lincolnnet.net/communities/joliet/joliet.htm

Access via:
I-55, I-80, and Rt. 30, 6 and 52, I-88 or I-355.

HISTORY

In 1673, two French explorers, Jesuit missionary Father Jacques Marquette and fur trader Louis Joliet, set on a journey to discover the interior of North America. The voyagers came through what is now Joliet and reported it as being fertile with a river, making it an ideal place for settlement.

157 years later in 1830, Robert Stevens and David Maggard made claims to Joliet and brought their families soon after. The city was officially founded in 1831, though, when Charles Reed built the first log cabin and settled in the area while it was still surrounded by

Potawatomi Indians. The area incorporated in 1852, the same year the Michigan Southern railway enabled a train to arrive in Chicago from the East.

Whether Joliet was named Juliet or Joliet is a matter not everyone agrees upon. Some say it was named after the explorer Louis Joliet.

We're #1! We're #1!

The first stoves manufactured in Illinois were made at Joliet's Adams Foundry.

Charles Mound at 1,235 ft. is the highest point in the state.

The first post office in Will County was located at Gougar Crossing. It became a stop on the way to Chicago and was nicknamed the "Dutch Inn" because everyone was very friendly. It is still being preserved by the Gougar family at the corner of Rt. 30 and Gougar Rd.

From 1875-1886 22 Will County men were issued patents for 35 different forms of barbed wire: farmers needed an abundant yet cheap supply of fencing to keep the cattle from feeding on their crops. Although Illinois's DeKalb County is the rightful birthplace of the wire, Joliet was its major producer and became known as "Barbed Wire Town" in the 1880s. There were more than 19 local manufacturers of the wire in 1874, and Joliet was possibly the third largest area for the fabrication of barbed wire in the country.

Joliet Junior College
1216 Houbolt Ave.
815/729-9020
Joliet Junior College was the nation's first junior college. Today it is one of 19 colleges nationwide to have received a national Medallion Award for student development.

Route 66 Raceway
3200 S. Chicago St.
815/722-5500
http://www.rt66raceway.com
Route 66 Raceway was the first stadium of drag racing.

Others claim that in 1834 John Campbell, the first postmaster, named it Juliet after his daughter, but that then-president Martin Van Buren, while in the area in 1845, made them change it to Joliet to match the name of the Joliet Mound. This is the same mound where Kinegoo, head chief of the Illinois tribe, stabbed Chief Pontiac of the Ottawa Indians in 1769.

Whatever you call *Joe-lee-ette*, do not call it *jolly-ette*, as this is against the law within city limits.

One fact agreed upon is that Joliet has acquired numerous nicknames throughout the years. In the mid 1800s, the city's quarrying industry flourished, employing thousands of people and earning Joliet the title of "Stone City" for its numerous limestone buildings. Joliet limestone was shipped as far as New York and has been used to construct the Rock Island Arsenal, Indiana and Illinois State Penitentiaries, and the Lincoln Monument in Springfield. By the late 1800s, the region's wealth of coal made Joliet a key location for the

Who's Who From Joliet

John Peter Altgeld (1847-1902) was the Democratic governor of Illinois (1893-1897) known for his pardon of anarchists involved in the Haymarket Riot.

Back before he put the cow in holy, Harry Caray was starting out his career at WJOL radio station along with Franklin McCormick.

Father Lawrence Martin Jenco was released from Lebanon in 1986 where he was held in captivity for 19 months. He was serving as director of Catholic Relief Services when captured by Muslim extremists. Thousands of people lined the streets to welcome him back to Joliet.

Did John D. Paige know that 141 years after he bottled flavored water under pressure (soon to be soda pop) that millions of people would suffer from "bloating?"

1943 Pulitzer Prize winner Martin Flavin hailed from Joliet.

steel industry and earned it the title of "Steel Town."

Today, The Chicago Ship Canal carries shipments of coal, fuel, and other resources from Joliet to the entire Midwest area. Joliet is a high-ranking industrial, railroad, and river-shipping center in Illinois.

TOURING

Buildings on the National Register of Historic Places

"At last! A theater to match my wardrobe"—Liberace

Rialto Square Theater
102 N. Chicago St.
815/726-6600
The finest Chicago hotels and theaters pale in comparison to the architecture and design of the living work of art we call the Rialto Theater. The doors to this tremendous building first opened in 1926—before radio and television captivated its audiences—and to this day it remains one of the last standing theaters of the vaudeville era. Designers C.W. and George Rapp who also created the Chicago, State/Lake, Oriental, and Granada theaters worked

Joliet's Who's Who in the Performing Arts

Lionel Richie wasn't so "easy" to beat on the varsity tennis team at Joliet Township High School.

In 1927, Loise Delaner became the first Illinois contestant to win the Miss America title.

Nora Bayes, a singer and a member of Ziegfeld Follies, was born in Joliet in 1880. One of her well-known songs is her 1918 remake of "Over There." Oh by gee, by gosh, by gum, by Jove, she also sang "Oh, By Jingo."

Charles Crusoe and his orchestra rocked Joliet with "I've Got Rhythm" and "Moon Glow."

Katherine Dunham studied dance and culture in the West Indies, which helped her develop her own technique. She has worked with many dance and opera companies as well as appeared in and choreographed many movies. There is a Katherine Dunham Museum and Children's Workshop at the Southern Illinois University.

As the World Turns soap star Kathyrn Hays graduated from Joliet Township High School in 1952 and went on to attend Joliet Junior College.

on the Rialto along with Eugene Romeo, whose designs can be seen in Chicago's Civic Opera House, Shedd Aquarium, and Wrigley Building.

The theater's architecture reflects Italian Renaissance, Byzantine, Roman, Greek, Rococo, Venetian, and Baroque influences and contains some of the finest replicas of early European design seen anywhere. The Grand Hall resembles the Hall of Mirrors in France's Palace of Versailles. 18 Corinthian style columns surround the rotunda, recalling the Pantheon in Rome. Hovering over these breathtaking recreations is the famed "Dutchess," the largest hand-cut crystal chandelier in the U.S.
Tours are given Tues. at 12:45 p.m. for $3.

Joliet Township High School
201 E. Jefferson
Besides a stunning Tudor Gothic exterior, Joliet Township High School boasts some spectacular student achievements. Its instrumental group won so many national band contests that they were banned from competing. In 1906 the graduating class presented the school with murals by William Henderson depicting Joliet and Marquette among the Indians.

Union Station
50 E. Jefferson
815/727-9279
815/727-9753
Joliet's awesome Union Station was built in 1912 and serves as the crossroads of three national train lines. Like Chicago, Joliet in 1991 completed a renovation of its run-down Union Station. A large mural, "Visions of Joliet" by Alejandro Romero, decorates the inside wall. The colorful painting depicts people, architecture, and events in Joliet's history. A larger mural entitled "Steam Train" by Kathleen Farrell and Kathleen Scarboro, which can be seen outside the station, depicts travelers at the station from years gone by.

Can Nester Come Out and Play?

Jacob Henry Mansion
20 S. Eastern Ave.
815/722-2465
If this mansion isn't the perfect setting for "Mystery in the Mansion" then I don't know what is. This dinner theater event which relies on audience participation currently runs from November to January. The home is also available for weddings, receptions, and parties.

Other Interesting Sites

St. John's School
404 N. Hickory
815/727-4788
Traditional tales attest that Abraham Lincoln made a speech in Demmond's pasture near what is now St. John's school on October 8, 1856.

St. Patrick Parish
710 W. Marion
815/727-4746
St. Patrick, established on November 16, 1838, is the oldest church in the Joliet Diocese and the second oldest Roman Catholic Church in the metropolitan Chicago area.

Will County Courthouse
14 W. Jefferson
On Oct 8, 1900 Theodore Roosevelt addressed a crowd of 3,000 at the old Will County Courthouse. An article written around the turn-of-the-century stated, "the courthouse symbolizes determination and stability and the fact that when neighboring counties built with logs and frames Will County built with brick and stone." The old courthouse was torn down to make way for the new one (c. 1969). However, The Will County Memorial monument, which commemorates the soldiers and sailors of Will County, stands on the exact site of the old courthouse.

St. Peter's Lutheran Church
310 N. Broadway
815/722-3567
During the Blackhawk War of 1832, Fort Nonsense was built where present day St. Peter's Lutheran Church stands.

Oakwood Cemetery
1919 1/2 Cass St.
c. 1885
In 1928 students from the University of Chicago excavated the "Oakwood Mound," an Indian burial site in the cemetery, and removed 90 of the estimated 360 bodies buried there for observation and inclusion in the university's museum.

Besides the mound, the cemetery is known for some prominent people buried there, including Joel A. Matteson, the 10th governor of Illi-nois and founder of the Woolen Factory—Joliet's first important manufacturing industry; author George Woodruff; Revolutionary War Veteran Private John Cook; Colonel Fred Bennitt, who fought in the Spanish American War; Corporal William Roberts, who carried the orders for the "charge of the light brigade"; and Sir William C. Van Horne, who helped build Canada's western railroad.

Joliet Public Library
150 N. Ottawa St.
815/740-2660
This main branch of the Joliet Public Library is housed in a historic building (c. 1903) designed by Daniel Burnham, an American architect who emphasized steel frame construction in his pioneering designs for Chicago commercial architecture. Some of his masterpieces are Chicago's Rookery (1886), Reliance (1890), and Monadnock (1891) buildings. These accomplishments lead Burnham to the seat of chief of construction for The World's Columbian Exposition in 1893.
Mon. - Fri. 9 a.m. - 9 p.m., Sat. 9 a.m. - 4 p.m., Sun. 1 a.m. - 5 p.m.

Joliet's Who's Who in Sports

Rudy! Rudy! Dan "Rudy" Ruettiger, former Notre Dame football player and inspiration to all, attended Joliet Catholic High School.

George Mikan was a professional basketball player selected in an Associated Press poll in 1950 as the greatest basketball player of the first half of the 20th century. In nine seasons he scored 11,764 points in 520 regular games for an average of 22.6 points a game and 2,141 points in 91 championship games for a 23.5-point average.

Before he did the Superbowl Shuffle, former Chicago Bear Tom Thayer played on the championship Joliet Catholic football team.

Jim Catarello, former Golden Gloves boxer and Olympic referee, was an athletic trainer at Joliet Township High School.

Larry Gura, a former pitcher for the Kansas City Royals, graduated from Joliet East High School.

Frank Pantalone, dubbed "Stronger Than a Mule" for his ability to throw a mule, break baseball bats over his arm, lift 30 men, and break a 1000 lb. rock on his chest, performed shows of his strength while residing at 213 S. DesPlaines.

1900 Olympic silver medalist Merrit Griffin and baseball players Mike Grace, Bill Gullickson, and Mark Grant were all from Joliet.

The Joliet Area Historical Society
17 E. Van Buren St.
715/722-7003
Exhibits include early automobiles, Joliet brewery memorabilia, sports paraphernalia, military artifacts, and more.
Admission is free. Open Tues. - Fri. 12 p.m. - 3 a.m.

Pilcher Park Nature Center
Gougar Rd. near Rt. 30
815/667-4054
In 1921, the late Robert Pilcher donated 320 acres of land to the park district of Joliet (the land was once owned by Daniel Burnham, construction chief of the 1893 Chicago Columbian Exposition). Today the land is known as Pilcher Park and contains a nature center operated by the Will County Forest Preserve District. The center features exhibits of the area's natural history, plants and animals, an indoor aquarium, turtle pond, outdoor education programs, and special events; the park has picnic tables, trails, and a playground area.
Admission is free. Open Mar. - Oct. 9 a.m. - 6 p.m., Nov. - Feb. 9 a.m. - 4:30 p.m.

Bird Haven Greenhouse and Conservatory
Andrew Barber & Clarence Oberwortmann Horticultural Center
225 N. Gougar (Gougar Rd. and Rt. 30)
815/741-7277
Bird Haven offers a stunning presentation of plants and flowers in an Italian Renaissance-style greenhouse. The vivid red, white, violet, and orange flowers pose no second to the displays found in Chicago's Lincoln Park or Lake Geneva's flower gardens. The center is open all year long and presents special attractions during the holidays.
Admission is free. Open daily 8 a.m.- 4:30 p.m., including holidays.

F.S. Allen Residence
608 Morgan St.
Prominent architect Frank Shaver Allen designed Christ Episcopal Church and Joliet Central High School. His own residence has a Romanesque arch and a Queen Anne Tower on the corner that sets off the second floor.

Long after Shaver's death, strange events began occurring in the house: items went missing, strange objects appeared out of nowhere, rockers moved inexplicably, and electrical appliances turned themselves on. While residing in the house Frank had lost his wife during childbirth, and later lost a son as well. This piece of history lead subsequent owners to believe Frank, or a family member, was haunting the house. After many such reports, a parapsychologist investigated the home in 1979 and confirmed that it was indeed haunted.

The Auditorium Building
Clinton and Chicago St.
c. 1891
Designed by G. Julian Barnes, The Auditorium Building is considered one of Joliet's important downtown buildings. Elements of interest include the Romanesque entrance to St. John's Universalist Church at the same location.

The Illinois State Penitentiary/Stateville
1125 Collins St.
The Illinois State Penitentiary was built in 1857 and, in its day, was a model institution. Today it serves as the administrative offices for Stateville Prison, the largest penal institute in Illinois. At one time the B-House was the world's largest rectangular cellblock. Designers W.W. Boyington and D.W. Wheelock, known best perhaps for the Chicago Water Tower, created the penitentiary.

Like so many prisons, the early days saw primitive conditions with waste buckets, strict rules, and torturous punishments such as the "cat-of-nine-tails"—a whip with several narrow strips of leather used to beat the inmates until bloody. The prison was ridiculed for "letting" prisoners work, thus taking away jobs from law-abiding citizens. Nonetheless, following the Chicago Fire in 1871, the inmates worked full days; they baked 1,000 loaves of bread per day and cooked meat to send to the newly homeless. Construction for Stateville started in 1916 just five miles from the Old Joliet Prison. The newer facility was equipped with the modern amenity of flushing toilets, something Old Joliet Prison didn't install until 1956.

Some famous residents of the prison have included Roger Touhy (1898-1959), a.k.a. The Terrible, who was a gambling boss and bootlegger during Prohibition. Touhy was allegedly framed by the Capone gang for kidnapping John "Jake the Barber" Factor in 1933 and was sentenced to jail in 1934. Touhy, sentenced to 199 years, spent the years 1934-1959 in Stateville. In 1942 he coordinated the most daring daytime escape in prison history. He slugged the driver of an automobile parked behind the prison kitchen and, along with seven other inmates, took three guards hostage and stole two ladders which were used to climb the tower, allowing them to escape in yet another car. Ten days after the escape, the convicts were charged with failing to notify the draft board of an address change, thus allowing the FBI to join in on the hunt. J. Edgar Hoover and FBI agents captured Touhy in Chicago shortly after he robbed an armored car. After many appeals, Touhy was released from Stateville in 1959, but was shot down a few weeks later in Chicago.

John Wayne Gacy, a.k.a. Pogo the Clown, tortured and killed 33 men and boys in Chicago in the 1970s. He was put to death at Stateville on May 10, 1994. His last meal was KFC, shrimp, strawberry ice cream, and Diet Coke. Diet Coke? Why not go all out and order Caffeine Free Coke or just water?

Richard Speck, a.k.a. Prisoner C01065, was responsible for murdering eight nursing students on July 14, 1966 in Chicago. On December 5, 1991 he suffered a massive heart attack and died at Joliet's Silver Cross Hospital.

Portions of the "Blues Brothers," starring John Belushi (Joliet Jake, a.k.a. prisoner 7474505B) and Dan Aykroyd (Elwood), were filmed in Joliet and Stateville Prison.

Colonel John Lambert, a prominent Joliet businessman, was also the warden of the Joliet State Penitentiary in the 1870s. It's written that the prisoners staged a revolt during his reign to protest their dissatisfaction with the quality of the food; they refused to work and staged a "sit in" in the yard. Lambert, crowbar in hand, drove them back to their cells. Then, he closed all the doors and windows and ordered prison stoves turned all the way up. Wooden "toilets" remained in the cells, and the heat and its attendant stench lasted for 24 hours. Prisoners were so violently ill they couldn't eat for three days. Ironically, Lambert ordered the kitchen to provide better food.

The bodies of unclaimed convicts who passed away while incarcerated were buried at Monkey Hill at the northern end of the prison property. In the mid-1900s, residents near the cemetery claimed they could hear a ghost chanting Latin at certain times of the day. "The Singing Ghost of Monkey Hill" soon filled local papers. They discovered the groundskeeper had a habit of singing in Latin to keep himself company and the entire hubbub "died down."

Camp Erwin
Formerly the fairgrounds for the Will County Agricultural and Mechanical Association, this site became the military's "Camp Erwin" in 1861 when it served as a training ground for Civil War draftees from the Will County area.

The first Joliet man to volunteer for the war was Frederick A. Bartleson, a dedicated soldier to say the least, who would later raise Company A of the 20th Regiment and would earn the title of Major after the Battle of Fort Donelson. At the Battle of Shiloh he was badly injured and needed to have his left arm amputated, but that didn't stop him from becoming Colonel of the Illinois 100th Infantry. In a charge at the Battle of Chickamauga, Bartleson and a few others were taken to a prison in Richmond, Virginia. He was released eight months later and rejoined his regiment in Georgia. He was shot and killed later in the war at Kenesaw Mountain.

RECREATION

Joliet—A Midwestern Mosaic
Walking Tour
815/727-2323
Mural and architecture walking tours discuss sites from 1860-1935.

Inwood Recreation Center
3000 W. Jefferson St.
815/741-7275
The Inwood Recreation Center houses a 17,000-square-foot ice rink and a state-of-the-art aerobics floor, which is fully mirrored and equipped with an audio amplification system. After a vigorous aerobics class, head over to the McDonald's that is conveniently connected to the center.

Haunted Trails Amusement Park
1423 N. Broadway
815/722-7800
This year-round family amusement center has 14 acres of go-karts, miniature golf, batting cages, rides, and arcade games.
Open daily 10 a.m. - 12 a.m.

ENTERTAINMENT

Empress Casino
2300 Empress Drive
P.O. Box 2789
888-4-Empress
The Empress I and Empress II boatsoffer over 1,000 slot, video poker, and video Keno machines; blackjack; roulette; craps; mini-baccarat; Let It Ride; and Caribbean Stud Poker. The pavilion features three restaurants: Steakhouse Alexandria (fine dining), Cafe Casablanca (casual Mediterranean and American), and the Marrakesh buffet. Located across from the pavilion, The Empress Hotel is a 102-room facility featuring a variety of rooms and luxury suites, an indoor pool/Jacuzzi area, and exercise room. Shuttle service is available from the hotel to the pavilion. Empress has the highest payout for 25-cent machines at 92.07%.

Harrah's Joliet Casino
150 N. Scott St.
800-Harrahs
Harrah's has two boats, the Northern and Southern Stars, which leave at different times during the day for their tour down the Des Plaines River. The land pavilion has three restaurants, two lounges, a gift shop, banquet facilities, and live entertainment. While Empress has a better pay out for their 25-cent machines, Harrah's is the high payer on the 50-cent slots with a 92.84% average.

Lucky Joliet?

Is this a lucky town? Ironically, Joliet's very own, Phoenix Horseshoe Company was once the world's largest manufacturers of horseshoes.

FOOD

Chicago Street Bar and Grill
75 N. Chicago St.
815/727-7171
Be sure to dine in the historical atmosphere of the Chicago Bar and Grill while visiting downtown Joliet. The exposed brick walls, mahogany tables, and dim lighting lend the restaurant a perfect 1920s appeal. Reasonably priced lunches are served from 11 a.m. to 3 p.m. and include a house specialty, The Beef & Bird—a mix of roast beef, turkey, Monterey Jack cheese, and creamy onion sauce on French bread.
Sandwiches $3.25-4.50, salads $2.25-$4, and side dishes $.75-$2.50. Open Mon. 11 a.m. - 3 p.m., Tues. - Thurs. 11 a.m. - 8 p.m., Fri. 11 a.m. - 10 p.m.

Aurelio's Pizza
1630 Essington Rd.
815/254-2500
This facility is the largest Aurelio's location and has banquet rooms, the area's largest sports bar, 30 TVs, and outdoor dining. See description in *Frankfort*, p. 58.

Mia Figliai & Co.
Joliet Center
158 N. Chicago St.
815/722-6400
This trend-setting restaurant offers authentic Northern Italian cuisine and hosts live jazz and a piano bar on Friday and Saturday nights.
Open for lunch Tues. - Fri. 11:30 a.m. - 2 p.m., for dinner Tues. - Sat. 5 p.m. - 10 p.m..

David's Pasta
2006 W. Jefferson St.
815/744-5253
David's Pasta serves Southern Italian lasagna, sauces, and chicken.
Open Mon. - Thurs. 11 a.m. - 9 p.m., Fri. 11 a.m. - 11 p.m., Sat. 4 p.m. - 10 p.m.

Inside the Empress Casino

The Steakhouse Alexandria
815/744-9400
In between cruises why not try Alexandria's superb steaks, chops, fish, poultry, and seafood.
Open Tues. - Sun. 11 a.m. - 5 p.m.

Papa Geo's Family Restaurant and Pizzeria
4200 W. Jefferson St.
815/729-1822
Papa Geo's has some of the best pizza in Joliet. They also serve prime rib, gourmet pasta, and premium liqueurs at their piano bar.
Open daily 6 a.m. - 11 p.m.

Café Magnolia
815/774-0082
150 N. Chicago St.
Café Magnolia's interior has golden walls with flowerpots hanging like picture frames. The wall is painted to look like exposed bricks with vines growing out of them in certain areas to give diners the feeling of eating in an old, hidden outdoor garden. You can dine inside or outside or order carryout. Sandwiches running $4.50 - $5.50 include tuna and veggie. A good alternative are the salads served in flowerpots ($2.50).
Open Mon. - Fri. 7 a.m. - 3 p.m.

SHOPPING

Chicago Street Mercantile
178 Chicago St.
815/722-8955
Looking for furniture new or old? You definitely want to check out this store first. Not second, not third—first! Their antique furniture dates from the 1800s to early 1900s, with its condition being mint to near mint. Some items for sale on our latest visit included an 1880 pump organ ($375), a 1930s dresser ($135), a 1910 pine bookcase ($575), an 1880 Victorian dresser with marble top ($1,250), and an 1890 mahogany chair with original upholstery ($350). Don't forget about such accessories as antique bottles ($2-$20), Tiffany-style

lamps ($400), or an antique trunk ($40).

JUSTICE

Just The Facts

Justice
Home to One of America's Favorite Ghost Stories

Resurrection Mary

Resurrection Cemetery
7200 S. Archer Ave.
312/767-4644

One cold night in 1934 on her way home from the Oh Henry Ballroom (now the Willowbrook Ballroom), a young woman died in a car accident on Archer Avenue. Legend states this young woman was a Polish girl named Mary Bregovy.

The first sighting of "Resurrection Mary" occurred in 1939 when a cab driver claimed to pick up a young woman wearing a white dress on Archer Avenue. The girl jumped in the front seat and asked him to continue north on Archer, telling him to stop as he passed Resurrection Cemetery. There she vanished—perhaps the first ghost to commit a crime by skipping out on the cab fare. Since then Mary has bummed rides from many young men, only to disappear in front of the cemetery. Some of these Romeos even claim to have kissed her and describe her lips as ice cold.

We're #1, We're #1!

The stained glass window in the Resurrection Mausoleum was once the world's largest stained glass window.

In 1977, passers-by spotted a young woman in a white dress grasping the bars of the cemetery gate and believed she was trapped inside. The police found no one on the grounds; however, two gate bars had handprints etched into the iron. Upon analyzation, it was determined that the handprints were made with extreme heat.

To this day, sightings of Mary still occur, and the stories still abound.

KANKAKEE

TOURING

Kankakee County Historical Society Museum
801 S. 8th Ave.
815/932-5279
The museum complex consists of the Main Gallery; the Taylor School, a one-room school built in 1904; Small Memorial Home, built in the 1800s of native limestone; a Newspaper and Print Shop; a permanent collection of Indian Artifacts; the Centennial Room; and the George Grey Barnard Wing with Towering Sculptures.
Admission is a $1 donation. Open Mon. - Thurs. 10 a.m. - 4 p.m., Sat. - Sun. 1 p.m. - 4 p.m. Closed Fri.

Indian Burial Mounds
Probably the most popular of all the mounds is located on the border of the Will-Grundy county line on the Dan Fisher farm. The Fisher Mounds, as they are called, were thoroughly excavated by the University of Chicago in 1929. Several hundred full skeletons were discovered, along with pottery and artifacts that can be seen in the museum of the Anthropology Department at the University of Chicago.

Trivia

The Illinois River starts where the Kankakee and Des Plaines rivers meet.

Kankakee is the center of the large-scale production of gladiola.

RECREATION

Bird Park
801 W. Station St.
815/939-9274
Established in 1927, this 23-acre park has a playground, fishing pond inhabited by plenty of duck and geese, a walking trail, boat ramp,

On the National Register of Historic Places

Oldest Building in Kankakee

Lemuel Milk Carriage House
165 N. Indiana
Built in 1860, this facility is now used for weddings, banquets, and meetings.

Warren Hilcox House
687 S. Harrison

Charles E. Swannell House
901 S. Chicago Ave.

Kankakee Street Hospital Historical District
100 E. Jeffery St.

band shell, picnic area, field house, and paddle boat rental.
Open dawn - dusk.

FOOD

Germ Free

Carlo's Restaurant
2060 W. Station St.
815/932-2924
Carlo's prepares excellent homemade breakfasts, lunches, and dinners and are famous for their jumbo pork tenderloin sandwich. They've recently won the Kankakee County Sanitary and Healthful Conditions Award two years in a row. (Note to self: get a list of restaurants that didn't win).
Open Mon. - Sat. 6 a.m. - 9 p.m.,
Sun. 7 a.m. - 2 p.m.

Famous Who's Who

Fred MacMurray, leading man and star of *My Three Sons*, was from Kankakee.

LANSING

Just The Facts

Village of Lansing
"Proud of Our Past"
25 miles south of Chicago

Population:

1990	28,131
1994	29,396
2010	31,416

Contact:
Village Hall 708/895-7200

Access via:
I-80/94

TOURING

On the National Register of Historic Places

Ford Airport Hangar
Glenwood-Lansing Rd. and Burnham Ave.
The hangar was built in 1926 for Henry Ford.

Lotton Art Glass Gallery
1938 17th St.
708/474-4022
The Lotton Gallery features beautiful art glass, which has been decorated using old-fashioned methods.
Open Mon. - Fri. 9 a.m. - 5 p.m.

RECREATION

Hollywood Park
2635 Bernice Rd.
708/474-8989
Hollywood Park offers two large, newly-remodeled 18-hole miniature golf courses, hundreds of arcade games, an outdoor cafe, a 50s style restaurant, go-karts, Cooter's Treehouse, batting cages, and more.
Open Sun. - Thurs. 12 p.m. - 10 p.m., Fri. - Sat. 12 p.m. - 11 p.m.

LODGING

For affordable overnighters:

Fairfield Inn
17301 Oak Ave.
708/474-6900
Free local calls, free breakfast, free HBO, and pay-per-view.

Holiday Inn
17356 Torrence Ave.
708/474-6300
But a mile from the Indiana border...

LEMONT

Just The Facts

Village of Lemont
"Village of Faith"

Median Age	32.7
Median Family Income	$49,044
Average Sale Price of Home	$212,022
Median Household Income	$42,658

Population:

Village	9,586
Twsp.	4,865
Total	14,451

Contact:
Village Hall 630/257-2532

Access Via:
I-55

HISTORY

Six years after the planning of Chicago at the site of Fort Dearborn in 1830, Lemont was settled, making it one of the oldest Chicago Southland communities. Prior to that time it served as a minor trading post. The name itself derives from *la mont*—the mountain—since the area sits on top of wooded hills.

Lemont was founded during construction of the Illinois & Michigan Canal, which was designed to link the Great Lakes to the Mississippi

River. It is said that Lemont owes its existence in some part to our great president Abraham Lincoln due to his tireless efforts to raise funds for the completion of the I & M Canal. Ironically, Lincoln passed through Lemont but once—on May 2, 1865 when his funeral train slowed from a speed of 20 m.p.h. to 5 m.p.h. so that residents could pay their respects.

Lemont's historic downtown—with its antique shops and old-

Famous Who's Who of Lemont

Flying Ace Rudy Kling built his plane "Jupiter: Pride of Lemont" at 312 Canal Street. The little red speed plane with a wingspan of 16 feet and eight inches helped him win the 1937 Cleveland air races and become a national hero. Kling fought to let a youngster, whom other racers felt was irresponsible, fly in an upcoming race. Ironically, the youngster struck Kling's plane and killed him, only three months after his victory in Cleveland.

Author Ralph Paine, an adventurous newsman during the Golden Era of Hollywood, was born in Lemont in 1871.

Miracle Worker?

Many claim Mother Mary Theresa Dudzik, a candidate for sainthood who died in 1918, was a miracle worker who healed the critically ill. The Polish immigrant, who in 1894 formed the Franciscan Sisters of Chicago, lived in poverty and cared for the poor and elderly. That very order received thousands of letters claiming they were granted favors through Mother Theresa. Her site in the Our Lady of Victory Convent in Lemont is the site of many novenas and the destination of many pilgrimages. Two nuns, once stricken with cancer, say they were cured after praying to Mother Theresa. A 17-year-old Chicago man awoke from a coma and regained partial limb usage after his mother prayed to the soon-to-be-saint. The stories go on and on. If granted sainthood, she would be Chicago's second saint. The first is Mother Frances Xavier Cabrini, an Italian-born nun who established orphanages, hospitals, and schools in Chicago.

fashioned restaurants attracting many visitors—and the nearby canal are a focal point of the town and attract many visitors.

On the National Register of Historic Places

Lemont Historical Society
306 Lemont St.
708/418-1700
In 1861, the Old Methodist Episcopal Church was built of broken pieces of Lemont stone, which you'll notice, while standing on the front steps, are mismatched and put together in a not-so-neat fashion. Inside, the church, like a peacock with its feathers, proudly displays a set of stained glass windows that were imported from Italy in the 1890s.

Today the building is home to the Lemont Historical Society and Museum, though it once served as a recruiting depot during the Civil War. Local tales say General Grant once stopped by to make a speech to boost morale during the Civil War. Museum exhibits re-create a schoolroom, an old-fashioned general store, an opera house with formal clothes, a doctor/dentist's office with tools, a newspaper printing room, and a jail. Farm machinery, wartime artifacts (including a calvary saddle used in the Civil War), and even a rag doll that survived the Chicago Fire are also on display.
Donations for admission appreciated. Open Thurs. - Fri. 10 a.m. - 2 p.m., Sat. - Sun. 1 p.m. - 4 p.m. year round. Also open Tues. 10 a.m. - 2 p.m. May - Oct.

Trivia

Let's see how well you know your Chicago trivia.

Chicago's oldest building was constructed of Lemont limestone in the late 1800s. What is the name of the building? If you answered the Water Tower, you're right. If you said anything else, you're wrong. For your lack of knowledge on the SS you must buy five copies of this book and pass them out to your friends.

I'll give you one more chance to gain some respectability. Can you name another well-known building that was built with Lemont limestone? Answer: The Congressional Library in Washington, D.C.

Since most of the cut stone from Lemont quarries moved via the I & M Canal and later via the railroads, it is only fitting that many structures along these transportation ways are made of its cut stone. The pamphlet "History of Cook County" estimates that the income from the quarries in Lemont during the 1870s amounted to 2.5 million dollars per year.

TOURING

The I & M Canal, DesPlaines River, and the Sanitary Ship Canal all flow through Lemont. These waterways along with the hilly terrain of the DesPlaines River Valley provide some of the most picturesque views in the Southland. Take a walk on the State Street Bridge to enjoy vistas of the town and river. This is the same river that Father Jacques Marquette and Louis Joliet traveled in 1673 when the region belonged to France.

- ***Oldest Church Building in the Area***
- ***First Catholic Elementary School***
- ***"The Shrine of the Poor Souls"***

St. James at Sag Bridge
107th and Archer Ave.
630/257-7000
St. James Catholic Church (est. 1833) and its adjoining cemetery,

St. James Sag.

which contains burials as far back as 1816, have long been rumored to be haunted. Both were established when America was only on its fourth president, though reports of hauntings didn't occur until 1847.

Are you familiar with Latin? If so, please go to St. James Sag Cemetery and translate what the monks are chanting. Don't be intimidated by the fact that they are 400 years old and float on air. We haven't read one report (yet) that they bite, hit, or even tease, so you'll probably be fine.

Unknown Soldiers of War Memorial

Danish Cemetery
127th St.

You wore a suit of faded khaki
To us a mantle of blue
Proudly we hailed you and whispered "Buddy"
We'll find a name and a grave for you

—Anna Doolin Rieck

The sight of a "floater" (the term used for a drowned body in the canal) was all too familiar to residents of Lemont in the early years. When one was spotted, the routine procedure entailed contacting the authorities, taking the body to the funeral home, and contacting relatives from IDs on the corpse. However, on July 1, 1919, the drowned body of a young boy in full uniform returning from WWI drifted down the canal bearing no identification, and no one came forward to claim him. Lemont treated him to a burial with full military honors, and the youth remained in an unmarked grave for 12 years until a war memorial for unknown soldiers was erected in 1932.

Spitting, Cowboys Who Don't Bathe, and Horse Poop in the Road

Smokey Row

Between River St. and the I & M Canal

Home to 100 saloons and gambling houses with "ladies" as permanent residents of the casinos and a center of much crime and uproar, in 1892 Smokey Row bragged of being the meanest street in America. One infamous gang, comprised of roughly 20 young men who claimed Lemont to State Street as their turf, infested the area and called themselves the "Hot Air" gang. The group earned the name "hot air" because their activities consisted mostly of insulting women who passed by and forcing them off the sidewalks. Because the town's undertaker was located on the same street, residents had to endure a flood of insults from loitering gang members as they made their way to bury their loved ones. The gang and their shenanigans ceased to exist when a police officer "accidentally" shot the leader. Soon after, in 1906, the last establishment on Smokey Row shut down. It is said that Frank Capone once resided in the Anderson Building on Stephen and Talcott.

Indian Trails

While touring Lemont and other SS areas, you will more than likely end up on Archer Avenue (171) somewhere along the way. This road runs on a frustrating angle because it was not meant to be a road, but an Indian path.

Alton/Legion Park

Main St./ New Ave./ Lockport St.

The Alton/Legion Park is dedicated to those Lemont residents killed while in the line of duty and stands on a triangular plot of land where the 1885 quarry strike "massacre" occurred. On May 4th of that year, the Illinois Militia was sent to Lemont to force striking workers to return to their jobs. Three Lemont residents died as a result of the strike.

The Lemont Post Office

42 Stephen St.

The post office, a product of the 1930s Art Deco era, houses a Charles Turzak mural representing Lemont's pioneer families that was dedicated in 1937. Turzak's works can also be seen at the Main

Post Office in Chicago and on the University of Chicago campus.

Lemont Village Hall
416-418 Main St.
630/257-1550
All mayors of Lemont have held office in this Romanesque building since its construction in 1893. Being that it was almost 100 years old, the Village Hall decided to remodel the inside in 1991, and the architecture is now an eclectic mix of old and new. On display is the self-guided photo exhibit, *Lemont and Its People,* assembled by the historical society.
Open Mon. - Fri. 8:30 a.m. - 5 p.m., Sat. 9 a.m. - 12 p.m.

Camp Sagawau
12545 W. 111th St.
630/257-2045
The Forest Preserve District of Cook County's Camp Sagawau is an educational center affiliated with Governors State University that provides vocational workshops and encourages the study of nature. The staff hosts guided walks and field trips that teach participants about the surrounding natural world, birds, fossils, and other topics.
Open Mon. - Fri. 7 a.m. - 3 p.m. Open for cross-country skiing in the winter.

Filming Site of Steve McQueen's Last Movie, *The Hunter*

Cookie Jar Museum
Alex Anderson Building
111 Stephen St.
Lemont, IL 60439
708/257-2102
Over 2,000 different cookie jars, some of which belonged to famous people, make their home in this unique museum. The only bad part is that all the jars are empty! The building was once known as Oldne Hall in honor of the Scandinavian god of war and poetry.
Hours are hit or miss.

Freehauf Building
107 Stephen St.
Over 100 years old, the Freehauf Building has seen many businesses come and go, but perhaps the most exciting time it had was being a

bookie joint and still in 1925. Unfortunately the fun didn't last long, and workers took off right before a sheriff's raid. One of various distinctive features of this stunning relic is its stamped metal ceiling.

Pacific Tall Ships Co.
106 Stephen St., Suite 100
800/690-6601
http://www.pacific-tall-ships.com
In this day and age of computer automation and technology, few things make us stand back and look in amazement at what the bare hand can do. The Pacific Tall Ships Co. handcrafts wood sailing ship models to the T, and their prices—ranging from $650 to $13,000—reflect that artistry. The store resembles a museum, with most of the boats encased in glass and labeled with plaques telling the boat's tale. Some of the ships commanding these princely sums include *The Sovereign of the Seas*, which was built by King Charles I in 1637 ($13,000); *The Wasa*, the finest warship Sweden had to offer in the 17th century ($8,625); *The Flying Fish* ($2,500); the *HMS Bounty* ($2,500); the *USS Constitution* ($4,500); and the *HMS Victory* ($6,500). Other unique items in the store: brass ship bells ($123.90), desktop chart magnifiers ($44.50), a captain's desk lamp ($165.90), box sextants ($179.50), and items from the captain's private collection, which are for display only.

RECREATION

Cog Hill Golf Country Club
119th St. & Archer Ave.
630/257-5872
Four 18-hole golf courses at Cog Hill are open to the public. One of them, Dubsdread, is the home of the PGA's Western Open and is listed by *Golf Digest* as one of the top 100 most challenging courses in the U.S.
Rates run $30 for 18 holes during the week, $35 on weekends. Carts are $29 extra. Lessons are available with a pro for $30-$55 per half hour.

FOOD

Brandt Cellars International
111 Stephen St.
630/257-9038
Brandt Cellars is a cute store wallpapered with bottles of wine. The owners are wine representers who exclusively sell 400-450 different wines—90% of which are all natural. Ever dream of having your name on a bottle of wine? Brandt Cellars offers custom labeling in addition to specialty items like great gift baskets, humidors, cigars, and 1920s tequila gift sets.
Open Mon. - Thurs. 11 a.m. - 7 p.m., Fri. 11 a.m. - 8 p.m., Sat. - Sun. 11 a.m. - 5 p.m.

The Mashed Potato Club of the Burbs

The Strand Cafe
103 Stephen St.
630/257-2122
The Strand started as Lemont's first antique store, but serves genuine New Orleans food in its current incarnation. The Strand appeals to all five senses: bright orange booths and funky ceiling images painted by a Michaelangelo wanna-be entice the sight; live accordion music involves the ears; the colored, misplaced streamers on the walls make one want to touch (and tear them down). Smell and of course taste are teased by a menu with items like barbecued alligator meat, jambalaya, and jumbo barbecued shrimp.
Menu items $5-$29.95. Breakfast served Sat. - Sun. 8 a.m. - 2:30 p.m.; lunch served Sun. - Thurs. 11 a.m. - 9 p.m., Fri. - Sat. 11 a.m. - 5 p.m.; and dinner served Sun. - Thurs. 11 a.m. - 9 p.m., Fri. - Sat. 11 a.m. - 10 p.m.

Montiferori's
11250 S. Archer Ave.
Gorgeous European gardens, a lake with black and white swans, swaying willow trees, and exotic animals make this historic estate a memorable place to hold a reception or wedding.

Lemont House
210 Main St.
630/257-3080
The Lemont House is known for having the best Korean cuisine around. They offer free soup with every lunch special for those who dine in.
Open Sun. - Mon. 11 a.m. - 9 p.m., Wed. - Sat. 11 a.m. - 10 p.m. Closed Tues.

AWL European Deli
12257 S. Walker Rd.
630/257-8322
Homemade bakery items, soups, pierogi, smoked Polish sausage, lunchmeats, and cheeses are only some of the good eats you'll find at AWL. Not only that, it's all reasonably priced: cabbage rolls run about $1.79/lb., Russian pierogi are $3.59/dozen, and smoked Polish sausage goes for $2.39/lb.
Open Mon. - Thurs. 9 a.m. - 7 p.m., Fri. 9 a.m. - 8 p.m., Sat. 9 a.m. - 6 p.m., Sun. 9 a.m. - 2 p.m.

Old Town Restaurant
113 Stephen St.
630/257-7570
Old Town's excellent European and American menu includes Polish, Lithuanian, Hungarian, German, Bohemian, and American dishes. They specialize in duck, breaded pork tenderloins, and dumplings and have a prime rib dinner special that comes with soup, potato, and desert for $7.50. Thursdays are all-you-can-eat pierogi dinners for $6.95, while Fridays bring all-you-can-eat-fish fries for $6.95. Be sure to try these other highlights at some point: a duck/pork plate ($8.50), the Lithuanian plate with kugels, potato pancakes, dumplings, and sauce ($7.95), a spicy beef goulash over potato pancakes ($7.95), and the stuffed cabbage ($6.50).
Open Sun. - Thurs. 11 a.m. - 8 p.m., Fri. - Sat. 11 a.m. - 9 p.m. Closed Mon.

Lemont Inn
324 Main St.
630/257-8925
The dimly-lit dining area, large winding wooden bar, fireplace, and assorted stuffed animals all give the Lemont Inn the feel of a lodge.

With its pool table and jukebox, the back room looks as if it belongs somewhere else. We suggest ordering as many appetizers as your table can eat—homemade onion rings; nachos with meat, cheese, olives, tomatoes, and onions; potato skins; jalapeño poppers; chili with cheese and onions—and feasting on those. However, you may wish to try one of the house's Lithuanian specialties or one of the $5.99 full dinner, weekend specials.
Open for lunch Mon. - Fri. 11:30 a.m. - 2 p.m., for dinner Mon. - Fri. 5 p.m. - 9 p.m.

SHOPPING

Canal Street Collectibles
307 Canal St.
Canal Street handles mostly fun new collectibles. Coca-Cola "memorabilia" right off the assembly line includes ornaments, magnets, trucks, tins, and radios. Betty Boop, Lucille Ball, Marilyn Monroe, Elvis, and Curious George all have their own cookie jars ($30+), salt and pepper shakers ($25+), lunch boxes ($10+), and other items. Products like a line of Madame Alexander dolls from the Fairy Tale Collection ($65), oriental thimbles of owls and birds ($5), scented soaps which had whole sunflowers, choo-choo trains, and teddy bears in them, and theme clocks depicting dolphins diving in the ocean or baby farm animals "horsing" around ($20) round out the store's treasures.
Open Tues. - Sun. 10 a.m. - 5 p.m. Closed Mon.

Antique Parlour
318 Canal St.
630/257-0003
Across the way from the Canal Street Collectibles and a world away in the aging department, the Antique Parlour draws its inventory from long gone decades. A sampling of recent sale items revealed an 1840s original Revival Sette with walnut wood and burgundy velvet upholstery ($950), a pre-1880 Queen Anne chair ($175), an 1880 original mahogany rocker ($295), brown spats ($36), a 1925 typewriter ($45), a 1940 Early Empire cherrywood dresser with the original knobs ($1,150), a Queen Anne 1920 walnut buffet ($595), a *Chicago Daily News* newspaper box ($25), old hotel soaps, David

Cassidy ephemera, baking pans, irons, china, Tinker Toys, vintage lace, cruet sets, silverware, books, paintings, and old magazines. They offer 20% off large furniture items plus a layaway plan. One of the best antique stores in the area!
Open Wed. - Sat. 11 a.m. - 4 p.m. Closed Sun.

Lemont Antiques
228 Main St.
630/257-1318
Lemont Antiques also has a large inventory and is another of the area's better antique stores. Besides an impressive selection of dolls and mantle and wall clocks, other very collectible offerings on our last visit included metal banks (monkeys on a see saw—$45), a 1913 Victor Victrola ($550), a Brunswick Victrola ($450), a 1910 Citronometer clock from a steamship ($400), a gorgeous red, velvet sofa from the late 1800s ($1,195), decanters ($20+), opera purses, beer steins ($27+), erector sets, cookie jars, an old pack of lifesavers, and salt and pepper shakers ($5+ for everything from tiki gods to monks to a squirrel holding two nuts). Dealers offer 10% off on higher-priced furniture and a 30-day layaway plan. They also repair clocks, shades, wind-ups, phonographs, telephones, and music boxes; rewire appliances; and duplicate missing parts.
Open daily 11 a.m. - 5 p.m.

Main Street Antiques Emporium
220 Main St.
630-257-3456
Check here for great bargains on vintage clothes, furniture, housewares, and knick-knacks. Some stand-out items on a recent visit included a 1930s dresser ($20), antique glass doorknobs ($20 each), lamps from occupied Japan ($70/pair), and turn-of-the-century women's shoes ($32/pair).
Open Tues. - Sun. 11 a.m. - 10 p.m.

Cleanest Antiques Around

Myles Antiques
119 Stephen
630/243-1415
Myles is a very clean, bright, and professional store with a large selection of antique and imported furniture. Besides clocks and newer items, you may find such unusual furniture pieces as a 1910

round oak table with claw feet ($795), a 1900 oak wardrobe from Ireland ($865), or an 1870s marble top walnut washstand from Scotland ($1,381).
Open Wed. - Sun. 10 a.m. - 4 p.m. Closed Mon. - Tues.

Don't Eat that Candle!

Me and My Sister Craft and Creations
203 Main St.
630/243-1769
You'll be talking about Me and My Sister long after you walk out the door. Their candles are truly one-of-a-kind and *look* good enough to eat! These candles come in the form of layer cakes ($40/with cake pan), pies, brownies, cup cakes ($4.50), and snickerdoodles ($11), which look like huge whipped cream balls. Votives with scents like orange, clove, and maple sugar are equally delicious. Country crafts like pictures, homemade birdhouses, yard stakes, and more are also for sale.
Open Mon. - Thurs. 10 a.m. - 5 p.m., Fri. 10 a.m. - 1 p.m., Sat. 10 a.m. - 4 p.m.. Closed Sun.

Ordinances You Need To Know About

Ordinance 8.16.020 Barberry Bushes Prohibited

It is unlawful to plant or permit growth or its varieties.

Ordinance 12.04.130 Playing Games on Public Ways

It is unlawful to play games upon streets, alleys, sidewalks, or other public places where they cause unnecessary noise or interfere with traffic or pedestrians.

(I don't think they uphold this as no children have been taken into custody for obstruction of pedway due to hopscotch.)

LOCKPORT

Just The Facts

City of Lockport
Homer Township
Township of Lockport
"City of Historic Pride"
"The City that made Chicago Famous"
35 miles southwest of Chicago

Median Family Income	$54,835
Median Age	32.7

Population:

1990	9,401
1994	10,386
2010	26,836

Contacts:
Lockport City Hall 815/838-0549
Chamber of Commerce 815/838-3557
http://www.lincolnnet.net/communities/lockport/lockport.htm

Access Via:
I-55, I-355, I-80, Rt. 171, Rt. 7, and Rt. 53

HISTORY

Armstead Runyon came to Lockport in 1830, the same year an American-made locomotive carried passengers for the first time. Seven years later, the area was chosen by the Illinois and Michigan Canal Commissioners to be laid out as a town specifically for them and the canal workers. During this time the area was called Runyontown, though Runyon himself changed it to the current "Lockport," and it was incorporated as such in 1853.

Lockport is a true canal city and home to one of the most historic waterways in the Midwest: the Illinois and Michigan Canal, which surged Chicago forward as a commerce center. Construction began shortly after Chicago was chartered as a town in 1833 and ended in 1848. The railroad followed shortly after, unfortunately leading to the demise of the canal as a transportation route.

Don't Bully that Bulldog!

Instigating a dogfight by gesture in Lockport can get you fined. Not only that, but it will let the rest of the town know that you really don't have much of a life.

Yet, the canal played a vital role in the area's development as it served as a means for pioneers to travel to the Midwest. This aspect of Lockport's history remains evident in the structures built of locally quarried stone (once flourmills, grain warehouses, and offices) along the canal's banks. Today the canal, which recently celebrated its sesquicentennial, is a beautiful walkway, bike path, and historic landmark.

On the National Register of Historic Places

Oldest Stone Building in Northern Illinois

Glady Fox Museum
9th & Washington
In 1837 this building served as the headquarters for the Illinois and Michigan Canal commissioners. Today it serves as the Glady Fox Museum and holds the distinction of being one of the oldest stone buildings in Illinois and the only stone building of its type in the nation. Exhibits include Indian artifacts and re-creations of a Victorian bedroom and a surgeon's office.
Admission is free. Open Mon. 11 a.m. - 3 p.m. & Fri. 11 a.m. - 3 p.m.

We're #1! We're #1!

At one time, Lockport was home to Isaac Merritt Singer, the inventor and manufacturer of the sewing machine.

Another Lockport area innovator, John Lane Sr., is said to have invented the first steel plow in 1835, the first of which he sold to Comstock Hanford of Lockport for $15.50. Since there was no steel manufacturing at that time in America, Mr. Lane had to cut the plow's individual pieces and weld them together. He never patented the plow and is documented as saying that if others could benefit by manufacturing it, then so be it. What a nice guy! Too bad Bill Gates doesn't share the same sentiment. 163rd St. and Gougar Rd. is the site of a steel plow made by the device's inventor.

TOURING

Lockport Gallery
200 W. 8th St.
815/838-7400
This gallery, a branch of the Illinois State Museum, presents a forum for the arts created by past and contemporary Illinois artists and artisans.
Open Tues. - Sat. 10 a.m. - 5 p.m., Sun. 12 p.m. - 5 p.m.

Gaylord Building
200 W. Eighth St.
815/838-4830
The Gaylord building (c. 1838) is one of the foremost historic sites in northeast Illinois. In its day, the building played many important roles in the region's commercial development. It has served variously as a depot for materials used to build the I & M Canal, a grain storage facility, a general store, a lock factory, a printing plant, and a plumbing supply house. Today it houses a visitors center, gallery, and tourism office.
Open Wed. - Sun. 10 a.m. - 5 p.m.

Norton Warehouse
10th and the I & M Canal
This massive structure, previously owned by Norton and Company, was once the backbone of Lockport's economy. The owners showed great foresight in recognizing that whoever had the capability to provide a warehouse and shipment facilities for grain on the I & M would have a formidable business. Today the empty building is all that remains of Norton's former empire.

Oldest Building in Will County

Pioneer Settlement
North Public Landing
8th to 9th Streets
803 S. State St.
815/838-5080
This outdoor, open-air museum showcases Will County Historical Society's collection of early buildings and artifacts. Some structures on display include a food cellar where food was stored for the winter, a pioneer school, mid-19th century houses, the Mokena village jail, an 1830s log cabin (Will County's oldest), an herb garden, a well, a smoking house, a kiln, and a railroad station depot.
Admission is free.

This 1830s log cabin is Will County's oldest structure.

RECREATION

Illinois and Michigan Canal Biking/Walking Path
It's hard to believe this narrow canal used to be the only waterway connecting Lake Michigan to the Mississippi. Today a path adjacent to the canal provides a scenic hiking and biking trail for everyone to enjoy.

Will County's First Designated Equestrian Trail

Spring Creek Preserve
South Bell Road, east of Rt. 52 on Cherry Hill Road
Homer Trails
815/727-8700
This 3.2-mile, 10-foot-wide trail runs through a predominantly rural area covered with brush and trees. Riders must obtain a bridal tag and pay annual permit fees, though the trail is free for skiers and hikers.
Obtain permits at the Forest Preserve District office in Crete, Joliet, Monee, or Romeoville. For Will County residents the cost is $5 for the permits and $15 for horse tags. Non-residents pay $10 and $30. Open dawn - dusk.

Trivia

Lockport volunteers in America's war with Spain were John Beck, Harry Dowse, Herman Schell, and John Norton, the latter of which served in Teddy Roosevelt's Rough Riders.

Ironically, John B. Preston, the first superintendent of the I & M Canal, accidentally drowned in it. He must have been supervising just a little too closely.

David Kennison, once a resident of Homer Township in the 1840s, was a member of the Boston Tea Party and had also fought at the Battle of Bunker Hill. Upon his death at 114 years of age, he was buried in Lincoln Park (then a cemetery) in Chicago.

Edward Poor, a veteran of the War of 1812, is buried in Lockport Cemetery.

ENTERTAINMENT

Bengston Pumpkin Farm
13341 W. 151 St. (between Bell and Parker Roads)
A haunted barn, hayrides, pig races, pony rides, farm animals, custom shop, concession stand, and—oh, yeah—pumpkins are what you'll find at Bengston Pumpkin Farm.
Admission is free for kids and $5.95 for adults. Open daily 10 a.m. - 8 p.m.

FOOD

Pastimes Café and Antiques
110 W. 10th St.
815/834-0993
This quaint café right off the I & M Canal trail offers homemade goodies such as blueberry, cranberry nut, and double chocolate

muffins; plain, blueberry, or onion bagels; and strudel stix; along with gourmet coffees served in carafes on antique trays. Sandwich options include homemade chicken salad, honey-roasted turkey, and brown sugar ham and egg salad. After ordering at the deli-style counter, you're free to sit anywhere in the café/antique store. While sitting
on the "merchandise," leisurely view the antique treasures such as china, vintage clothing, lamps, advertising memorabilia, old dolls, and toys surrounding you. They're all for sale.
Open Mon. - Fri. 6 a.m. - 3 p.m., Sat. - Sun. 10 a.m. - 5 p.m.

Anthony's Pancake House and Restaurant
1030 E. 9th St.
Lockport, IL 60441
815/838-2445
Besides the fact that your coffee cup will never run dry at Anthony's, its menu is chock-full of good eats. Choices range from thirteen different salads to New York strip steak, seafood, and ribs, with an array of sandwiches in between. If you're looking to really pig out for breakfast, or if you're in the "breakfast menu" mood, go here! It's hard to choose from among the gourmet pancakes, huge waffles, thick French toast, or many skillets. Trust me, whatever you decide, you can't lose! If you're a pancake or banana lover, go for the banana pancakes: the cakes are huge and a fresh layer of bananas is nestled in between each. The average meal with a drink runs about $10.
Open daily 6 a.m. - 10 p.m.

Public Landing
Located in the historic Gaylord Building (c. 1836)
200 W. 8th Ave.
815/838-6500
A singular, romantic dining experience awaits you at the Public Landing, which is located along the banks of the I & M Canal. A bread basket that proceeds the meal consists of corn muffins (good enough to make a meal out of) and hearth bread. The recommended Maryland crab and shrimp cake appetizer ($5.95)—a sweet meat patty served with a pineapple butter sauce—made me forget my seafood prejudices. Other appetizers include calamari with homemade tomato bread, jumbo prawns with BBQ butter sauce, and chicken livers with onions. Not a bad start at all.

Continue this bounty from the menu of about thirteen entrees and four daily specials. How about the grilled chicken with Canadian bacon topped with a barbecue butter sauce and accompanied by a salad and corn pancake, or the blackened filet of beef served with grilled banana peppers and a peanut sauce? It will be hard, but save room for desserts the likes of New Orleans bread pudding with whiskey sauce and cheesecake with fresh fruit.
Appetizers $4.95-$7.95, entrees $13.95-$19.95. Open Tues. - Fri. 11:30 a.m. - 9 p.m., Sat. 5 p.m. - 9 p.m., Sun. 4 p.m. - 8 p.m.

SHOPPING

Canal House Antiques
905 S. State St.
815/838-8551
Canal House deals in fine American furniture from the 18th and 19th centuries.
Open Thurs. - Sat. 11 a.m. - 5 p.m.

Antiques on State
901 S. State St.
815/834-1974
A good place to find European and American antiques and Victorian decorative arts, Antiques on State also specializes in 19th-century glass and china.
Open Wed. - Sat. 11 a.m. - 5 p.m., Sun. 12 p.m. - 4 p.m.

Prairie View Gallery
916 S. State St.
815/838-7480
A must see in Lockport! In its more than 1000 square feet, Prairie View displays the work of established regional artists—unique, attractive items perfect for gifts: handmade cards for weddings, bridal showers, and special events; artwork from abstract mixed media to pastels and watercolors; and other crafty items.
Open Wed. - Sun. Call for specific hours.

LODGING

Liberty Inn Bed & Breakfast
1225 S. Hamilton St.
815/838-5403
This Victorian bed and breakfast in a charming historic building makes the ideal home base for a weekend of antiquing.
$65-$85 per night.

SPECIAL EVENTS

Living History Performances

Pioneer Settlement
North Public Landing (8th - 9th Streets)
803 S. Sate St.
815/838-5080
Living history performances reenacting pioneer cooking, trades, chores, and transportation are given during Old Canal Days (below) as well as various times May through October. Call for details.

Old Canal Days
Historic Downtown Lockport
Third weekend in June
This annual event pushes the conventional level of fun and

Historic downtown Lockport, site of June's annual Old Canal Days.

excitement to unholy extremes, with carriage rides, a petting zoo, live entertainment, amusement rides, educational exhibits, crafts, a parade, baby contest, and yes—a beer garden.

Civil War Days
Delwood Park
1911 Lawrence Ave.
815/838-1183
Weekend following Labor Day
See what life was like before penicillin during a weekend of historical reenactments from the Civil War and portrayals of life in the 1860s. The event comes complete with authentic foods, costumes, and military uniforms.

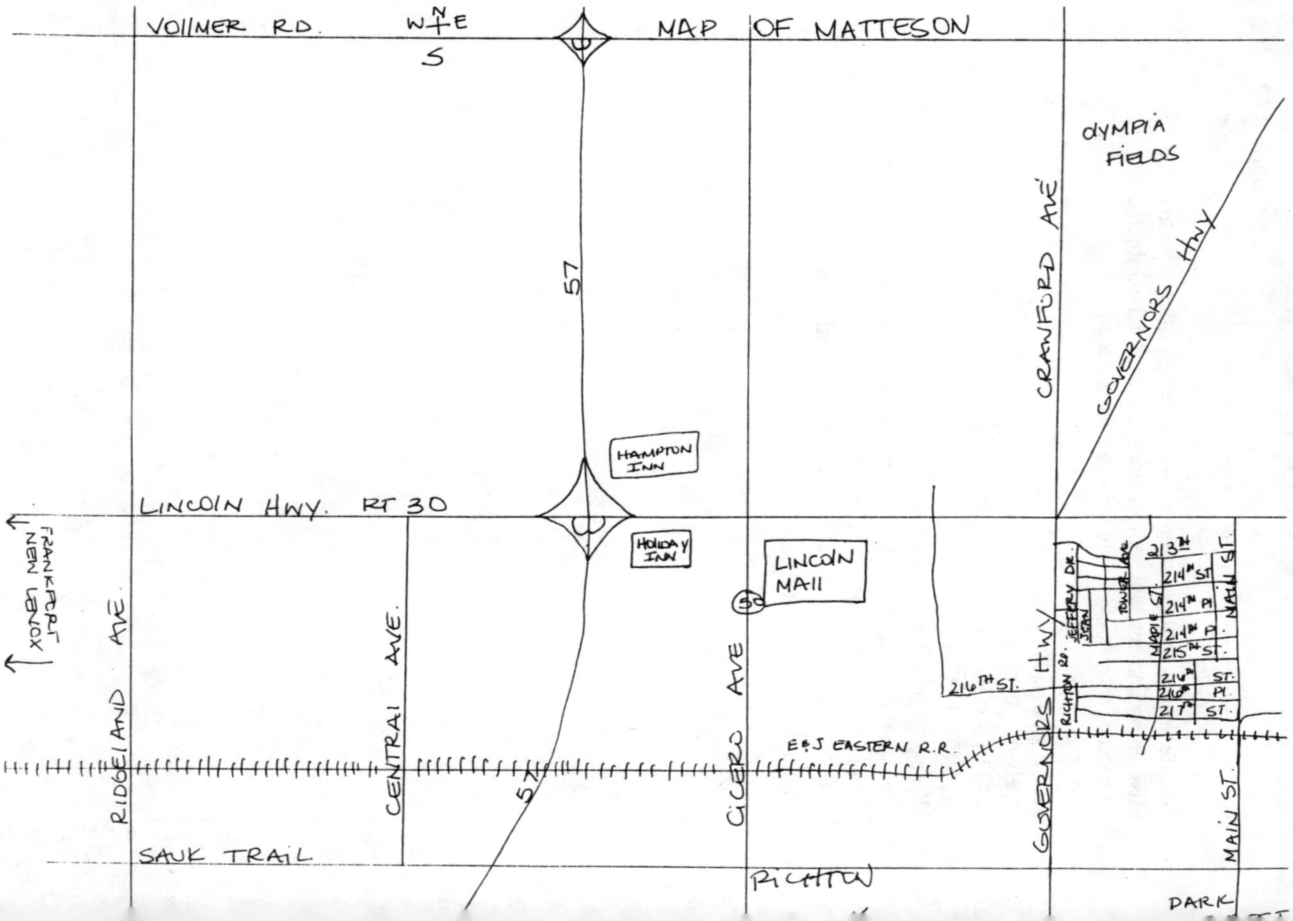

MAP OF MATTESON
N
W E
S
VOllMER RD.
LINCOlN HWY. RT 30
FRANKFORT
NEW LENOX
57
HAMPTON INN
HOLIDAY INN
LINCOLN MAll
50
CRAWFORD AVE
GOVERNORS HWY
OLYMPIA FIELDS
RIDGELAND AVE
CENTRAL AVE
CICERO AVE
SAUK TRAIL
RICHTON
E&J EASTERN R.R
216TH ST.
RICHTON RD.
JEFFERY DR.
JEAN
TOWER LANE
MAPLE ST.
213TH
214TH ST
214TH PL
214TH PL
215TH ST.
216TH ST.
216TH PL.
217TH ST.
MAIN ST.
MAIN ST.
PARK

Matteson

MATTESON

Just The Facts

Village of Matteson
"Crossroads of Heritage and Progress"
30 miles south of Chicago

Land Area	8 sq. miles
Median Age	32.3
Median Family Income	$51,833
Average Sale Price of Home	$117,286

Population:

1990	11,378
1994	12,389
2010	21,136

Contacts:
Village Hall 708/748-1559
http://www.lincolnnet.net/communities/matteson/matteson.htm

Access via:
Interstate I-57, I-80, 294, 394, Rt.30, and Cicero Ave.

HISTORY

Although the village was founded in 1855, it wasn't until April 10, 1889 that it was named after Joel Aldrich Matteson, an Illinois governor who introduced the first system of free schools to Illinois. As a young, predominantly German town, Matteson had not one, but three major railroads trisecting it: the Illinois & Central, the Michigan Central, and the Elgin & Joliet.

Matteson's biggest population growth occurred between 1970 and 1980 when it jumped from 4,741 to 10,225.

Matteson (pronounced Matt-e-son, NOT Matt-son), is one of the few suburban towns that really gets its undies in a bind if you mispronounce its name (the other being Joliet). Several years ago village officials went so far as to do a mailing to let residents know which was the proper pronunciation.

Making a weekly trek to Matteson has become a routine for most residents within 25 minutes of the town. Everything needed can be found within its 2.2 million square feet of shopping space, home to a large mall, grocery stores, outlet stores, a Target, a Walmart, a Best Buy, and a health club. It's also an alternate shopping location for residents who don't want to deal with the traffic of nearby Orland Park.

TOURING

Hahne Family House
3616 W. 216th
c. 1860
Built by William Hahne in 1860, this Victorian remains one of the oldest residences in the village, and its architecture has not been tampered with over the years. A structure behind the home was erected in 1914 and used as a slaughterhouse. William Hahne's daughter resided in the house until her death in 1974 at the age of 91.

Village Barber Shop
3612 W. 216th
c. 1896
The Village Barber Shop could be the poster child for that famous phrase, "once a barber shop always a barber shop," as they have been providing their services since 1896!

Maloni Tavern
3601 W. 216th St.
c. 1865
Built in 1865, this structure has operated as a tavern for 109 years of

its 133-year existence. It served shots and brews through the second term of Abraham Lincoln and has seen the aftermath of the Civil War, the birth of the nickel, and the addition of fourteen states into the union.

Ciao's
3613 W. 216th
c. 1880
In 1880, William Arnold erected the "Farmer's Hotel," consisting of a saloon, kitchen, summer kitchen, dining room, parlor, and bedroom, plus thirteen rooms upstairs for lodgers. The hotel is now home to Ciao's, a fine Italian restaurant.

Ciao's

The Nortmeir House
3735 W. 216th
c. 1894
The Nortmeir House remains virtually unchanged since local carpenter Henry Stege built this home in 1894. Stege's woodworking techniques and architectural touches—cleaner than the rough work typical of the day—put him ahead of his time, making this house a marker in Midwest architecture.

St. Paul's Evangelical Lutheran Church
6200 Volmer Rd.
c. 1883
For its 100th birthday, St. Paul's received the gift of restoration. And, even better, much of its original architecture was retained.

Unsolved Mysteries in Matteson

In 1980 a construction crew unearthed a gravestone with a name that has failed to surface in village records. Maybe you can identify the young girl:

Olinda Themer
Died in 1887 at the age of 2

On Feb 22, 1943 during WWII, Matteson experienced one of the worst fires in its history. A string of freight cars collided with oil cars when being switched onto the Illinois & Central Railroad tracks. According to stories, flames flew 100 ft. in the sky. To make matters worse, another line of freight trains crashed into the burning cars. It is said that remnants of this disaster can still be found, and local historians are looking for people who remember that day and can help piece together what happened. If you, or someone you know has information about either of these unsolved mysteries, please contact the Matteson Historical Society.

The Sieden Prairie School on the same site was built in 1869 and consisted of one classroom and two cloakrooms. Most children had to speak German on the first day to accommodate the major ethnicity in the area (as opposed to the seventh day, when they rested).

Henry Gross Home & Harness Shop
3624 W. 216th
In 1875, this building was used as living quarters for the Gross family as well as a harness shop. The building was sold and remodeled in the 1960s, though the original flooring still remains.

Matteson Historical Society
813 School Ave.
708/748-2326
Unlike at most museums, the excellent exhibits of the Matteson Historical Society are displayed in open spaces, making it easier to get a glare-free view. One exhibit, a vintage kitchen scene, includes historic stoves, pantry, irons and board, food containers, and hats and aprons; another is a "train car" com-plete with original signs, lug-

The trophy and an actual uniform from 1930 when the Matteson baseball team won the SS tournament are on display at the historical society.

gage, clothing, and other train items. Indian artifacts, tavern memorabilia, and farm equipment are displayed in additional settings. The extremely nice and helpful staff add to the pleasure of a visit here.

Admission is free.
Open Mon.-Sat.
1 p.m. - 3 p.m.

Illinois Central R.R. car # 9951 sits on a track in the Matteson Village Hall parking lot, and is dedicated to the Honorable Joseph Feehery, the village president for twenty-four years. He served from 1956 to 1981 and again from 1985 to 1986.

Elliotts, Elliotts, and More Elliotts

Elliott Cemetery
Rt. 30 one half mile East of Rt. 54
Welcome to the Elliott family cemetery. Its earliest burial was in 1850 (Franklin B. Elliot); its latest was in 1977 and is unmarked.

Tradition reports that Dana Elliott, an early settler and father of seventeen children, was a good friend of Abraham Lincoln and Stephan Douglas and accompanied them on their debates.

FOOD

Best Sports Bar in Matteson

Bocce's Sports Bar & Grill
3909 Rt. 30
708/748-8080
Bocce's is a fun atmosphere to be in whether you're hanging out at the bar with friends or enjoying a meal in the dining area. The menu offers a wide variety of items including catfish, shrimp, salads, dozens of sandwiches, patty melts, and other entrees. However, in the spirit of the energized sports bar atmosphere, I recommend ordering fun foods like taco salad, nachos, stuffed potato skins, and a basket of cheese fries. The taco salad is a huge, deep-fried tortilla basin of shredded lettuce, tomatoes, cheese, beef, and onions. You would have to search a long time to find a plate of nachos or a basket of fries bigger than what is served here.
Open Sun. - Thurs. 11 a.m. - 12 a.m., Fri. - Sat. 11 a.m. - 1 a.m.

J.N. Michael's
5000 W. 211
708/481-3364
J.N. Michael's flaunts a diverse menu with great prices, making it the perfect place to go when you don't know where you want to go. The atmosphere is family-oriented, warm, and friendly, good reasons why J.N.'s is probably the most popular restaurant in the area. A complete dinner can be had for under $9 and comes with a beverage, entree, potato, soup, and dessert. Some favorites include the chicken parmigiana, southern fried chicken, and roast turkey.
Open Sun. - Thurs. 6 a.m. - 11:30 p.m., Fri. - Sat. 6 a.m. - 1 a.m.

"World's Greatest Hamburgers"

Fuddruckers
300 Tower Center
708/747-7763

Fuddruckers proffers a nice selection of singular burgers and sandwiches such as lemon pepper chicken; ribeye steak; the Chula Vista burger with jalapeño jack, guacamole, and pico de gallo; the Broadie Oaks with Monterey, guacamole, and bacon; and the Downers Grove with cheddar, chili, and grilled onions. A large topping bar carries everything necessary to complete that sandwich or fries, including jalapeños and melted cheese. *Kids eat free Mon. - Thurs. after 4 p.m. Open Sun. - Thurs. 11 a.m. - 9 p.m., Fri. - Sat. 11 a.m. - 10 p.m.*

SHOPPING

Lincoln Mall
Managed by Lincoln Mall Management
208 Lincoln Mall
708/747-5600
Come for the 140+ stores and stay for the 5,500 parking spaces. Lincoln Mall, built in 1973, is anchored by major stores such as Carson Pirie Scott, JC Penney, Sears, and Montgomery Ward.
Open Mon. - Sat. 10 a.m. - 9 p.m., Sun. 11 a.m. - 6 p.m.

The Music Store
4314 W. 211th St.
708/748-0555
Shopping at The Music Store is all rhythm and no blues. Instruments, sheet music, books to teach yourself, and all the accessories—picks, strings, foot peddles, microphones, and band supplies—are well-stocked. Owner Rick Dewitt teaches lessons on various instruments from the guitar and banjo to the piano and drums. Bands looking for members can post notices on the bulletin board.
Open Mon. - Fri. 11 a.m. - 9 p.m., Sat. 10 a.m. - 5 p.m.

Sell it Again Sam
4330 W. Lincoln Hwy. (Rt. 30)
708/481-4999
I am very impressed with what the owners have done with this store over the years: It has taken on the feel of trendier antique malls in the city, but without the downtown price tags. Upon entering Sell It Again Sam's, patrons are immediately greeted by dressers, cabinets,

Traffic Tips

As soon as you exit I-57 and head east on Rt. 30, watch your speed. The speed limit is 40 m.p.h.

Considering how busy the area gets, traffic isn't too big a problem in Matteson. Yet, things can get a little tense between Cicero and Governor's Highway on Rt. 30 where all the stores are, and drivers can go a little crazy there. Keep your eyes W I D E open.

To avoid Rt. 30 all together, take Cicero to Sauk Trail or Volmer. Both provide close alternatives to the stop-and-go of Rt. 30.

coffee tables, end tables, futons, and kitchen sets. Lamps and other accessories sit on the tables; entire china sets are displayed in the china cabinets; new and old mirrors and art hang on the walls above the furniture. In the back near the cash register, a more cramped section contains old records, appliances, kitchen electronics, barware, and aging typewriters. Shelves display nicer porcelain figurines, barware, jewelry, and glass collectibles. When in the area and in need of furniture, make this a must-visit.
Open Mon. - Fri. 9 a.m. - 8 p.m., Sat. 9 a.m. - 6 p.m., Sun. 12 p.m. - 5 p.m.

Discount Records
Rt. 30 & Governors Highway
708/481-4550
See description under *Frankfort*, p. 68.
Open Mon. - Sat. 10 a.m. - 9 p.m., Sun. 11 a.m. - 5 p.m.

LODGING

Holiday Inn
708/747-3500
500 Holiday Plaza
This 204-room Holiday Inn is one of the nicer hotels located in the SS and has a convenient location off Rt. 30 and I-57. Don't think

of this as the average hotel with loud kids in floaters doing cannon balls in the pools and teens perennially glued to the arcade games. The Holidom has an indoor pool, miniature golf, fitness center, and game room. The Café de Plaza's award-winning Sunday brunches (especially popular for Mother's Day and Easter) include crepes and imported cheeses in their bountiful spread. Dinner highlights are the Friday night seafood buffet featuring crab legs and the Saturday evening prime rib buffet. Nightlife at the Holiday Inn can be found at The Atrium Lounge, which hosts live entertainment Tuesdays through Saturdays and offers complimentary appetizers weekdays from 4 p.m. - 7 p.m.

Brunch $16.95 adults, $14.95 seniors, and $7.95 children. Café de Plaza is open daily for breakfast and lunch 6 a.m. - 2 p.m.

MIDLOTHIAN

Just The Facts

Village of Midlothian
"Community that Pride Built...and Maintains"

Contacts:
Village Hall 708/389-0200
http://www.lincolnnet.net/users/lmidloth/template.htm

TOURING

Bachelor's Grove
Rubio Woods Forest Preserve
c. 1864
Be afraid. Be very afraid. I was. No, not afraid to go to the cemetery, but to make sure this cemetery was detailed to the satisfaction of the Southsiders. As Bachelor's Grove holds legendary status, then locals, by default, are expert parapsychologists.

This abandoned cemetery is said to have more ghost stories told about it than any other place in the Chicago area. Beyond mere tales, 100 paranormal occurrences have been reported there: unexplainable images in photos, ghost lights, voices, apparitions, and sighting "things."

The journey to this local institution starts with the narrow, eerie, tree-lined walk to the cemetery, which gives new meaning to the phrase, "getting started is the hardest part." I'm willing to bet many venturers ran scared before ever making it to the actual cemetery.

It is on this path that a phantom farmhouse supposedly reveals itself and quickly disappears. Witnesses all describe it the same: white house with porch pillars, a swing, and a soft light burning in the window; however, it is never reported in the same place.

Another frequent ghost sighting occurs near the lagoon next to the cemetery. During the days of Prohibition, Chicago mobsters used to dump their "undesirables" in that same lagoon.

The "White Lady" or "Madonna of Bachelor's Grove" is said to be the ghost of a woman buried in the cemetery next to her young son. On nights of the full moon she has been seen wandering the cemetery with a baby in her arms. (She must be suffering from agoraphobia, because when I was a kid the story went that she ventured out to the corner store and got a pint of milk for the baby.)

On my first trip to the cemetery before I had a clue of its reputation, a creepy feeling that we were not alone came over me while we were walking down that path, and I made everyone go back to the car. Be that as it may, Bachelor's Grove remains a popular place to go after parties. I just wonder how many stories are the fabrications of insobriety.

Scenes from the streets of Mokena: Little Al's Bar and Grill (*above*), Marley Church (*right*), and Marley Candies (*below*).

MOKENA

Just The Facts

Village of Mokena
"Planned Progress, Pleasant Living"
One of the lowest tax rates in the Chicagoland area.
35 miles southwest of Chicago

Area	4.5 sq. miles
Median Age	29.1
Median Household Income	$46,575
Average Sale Price of Home	$232,000

Population:

1990	6,128
1994	9,288
2010	9,942 (already surpassed)

Contacts:
Mokena Park District 708/479-1020
http://www.mokena.com

Access via:
I-80, Rt. 45, I-57, I-294, and I-55

HISTORY

Mokena is the spawn of the Rock Island Railroad and an early population of German, Irish, and Swiss immigrants. In 1852, nineteen years after the first settlers arrived, entrepreneur Allen Denny (no relation to the Denny's restaurant on 191st), a New York immigrant, authorized the sale of lots along the north side of the Rock Island tracks from Wolf Road to Mokena Street.

The census of 1930 reflected almost no population change from that of 1880. That's 50 years! Let's look at what the world was doing while time stood still in Mokena. For the first time America saw: electricity, the American Red Cross, the opening of the Brooklyn Bridge, the completion of the Washington Monument, the Haymarket Riot in Chicago, the dedication of the Statue of Liberty, free mail delivery, the first motion picture camera, the zipper, the Homestead Strike, the stockmarket Panic of 1893, the Chicago Fire, the use of X-rays, the modern Olympic Games, the Spanish-American War, the Model T, the Boy Scouts of America, the sinkings of the Titanic and Lusitania, the vote for women, World War I, Einstein's theory of relativity, and Prohibition.

Over the past decade (1988-1998), Mokena has finally made up for that standstill and continues to do so. It has more than doubled in population since 1990, growing from 6,100 to more than 12,600 residents. Almost overnight Mokena went from a quiet country town to one of the fastest growing areas of the Southwest Suburbs.

Today the exact literal meaning of the name "Mokena" is not known. History and tradition indicate that it is the Potawatomi word for "turtle"—which in English means reptile with a trunk enclosed in boney shell.

TOURING

Village's First Church

German United Evangelical Church of St. John's
Corner of Front and First streets
c. 1862

American Revolution Veteran

St. John's Cemetery
Wolf Rd./Front St.
Charles Denny (December 25, 1750 - August 6, 1839), a veteran of the American war for independence, is buried in St. John's Cemetery. He is just one of two Revolutionary War veterans buried in the area.

RECREATION

Imagination Station
Mokena Junior High
11331 W. 195th St.
708/479-3130
Imagination Station makes one want to be a kid again. This is not your ordinary playground—this is a kid's dream! Volunteers raised $100,000 in only five days to fund the 10,000-square-foot, one-of-a-kind playground. Anchored to the ground with 60 telephone poles and constructed of 17-foot towers, the station is finished with a dragon, mazes, swings, slides, space ship, and intercom that will keep kids busy for a long time to come.

Ski Trail
The Hickory Creek Preserve on LaPorte Road offers 2.5 miles for cross-country skiing with various access entrances.

Old Plank Road Trail
815/727-8700
The Old Plank Road Trail runs twenty miles from The Will County forest preserve of New Lenox to Chicago Heights with various entry points in each town. Mokena residents use the trail for biking, walking, and jogging.

ENTERTAINMENT

Wild Food Workshop
Environmental Learning Center
20851 S. Briarwood Ln.
708/479-2255
The Forest Preserve District of Will County offers an annual workshop which teaches participants how to identify and prepare wild plants for eating (yummy!). Part of the time is spent in the field identifying wildflowers; the rest of the time focuses on how to prepare such edibles and culminates with sampling from a wild foods buffet. *Held in May—rain or shine. Call for the specific date.*

The End of the World is Coming Soon. Drink Beer.

World's End
Right off I-80 and Rt. 45 down Old 191st
708/479-9600
This soon-to-open world of fun will offer over 800 beers as well as home brewed favorites from a full production brewery. Two world class chefs will provide an international menu for the restaurant and banquet hall. The 31,000-square-foot brewery and playground is due to open in May of 1999 and will allow customers to brew their own beer, make wine, play virtual reality games, shop in a huge liquor store containing hundreds of specialty liquors, or just hang out in the bar. The word is that World's End will attract fun seekers not only from the South and Southwest Suburbs, but also from Chicago and the Northern Suburbs.

FOOD

Foot Longs...Get Your Foot Longs

Mitchell's Steamboat
Intersection of Wolf Rd. and Rt. 30
815/469-4343
Is it a restaurant or a hot dog stand? The food is prepared too quickly to be a restaurant, no servers exist, and they sell hot dogs. Let's call it a restaurant with a hot dog stand appeal. Better yet, let's call it a "hot dogstaurant." This hot dogstaurant has a warm, family atmosphere with plenty of indoor booths and tables, as well as outdoor picnic tables. Everyone eats at Steamboat: it's one of those presumed, you-just-do-it sort of things, like breathing. Foot longs, hoagies, and tamales are in high demand among the patrons, although I like to order the beef sandwich (on a French roll with a generous helping of au jus and peppers—red sauce and cheese are extra) every now and then just to keep them on their toes. For variety, the menu also consists of jumbo, corn, chili, and cheese dogs; bratwurst; Polish and Italian sausage; chicken; hamburgers; Gyros, pizza puffs; salads; and the usual appetizers—onion rings, poppers, cheese sticks, and fried veggies.
Open daily 10:30 a.m. - 8:30 p.m.

Most In Tune With Customers

Nancy's Pizzeria
19803 S. LaGrange Rd.
708/478-8787

Nancy's has been rated the "Best stuffed pizza in Chicago" by the *Chicago Tribune*, *Chicago* magazine, and ABC-TV. Overshadowed by this mega-stuffed sensation and the popular deep-dish, Nancy's thin crust is often ignored and is definitely under rated. This delicacy has a well-baked, crunchy crust and cheese that keeps its white color when baked. If you haven't tried it you're missing out on a great pizza. The customer service is great too. Once when my father hadn't ordered a pizza there for about a month, the staff called to inquire if everything was okay.

Open Mon. - Thurs. 4 p.m. - 10 p.m., Fri. 11 a.m. - 11 p.m., Sat. 4 p.m. - 11 p.m., and Sun. 4 p.m. - 9 p.m.

Nick—Now There's a Name You Can Trust

Nick's Steakhouse
19634 LaGrange Rd.
708/479-4704

Nick's offers the best of both worlds. The restaurant delivers a fine dining experience with some of the best steaks served in the SS, while the lounge area remains a popular hang out for locals to kick back, play darts, and have a few drinks. Dinners ranging from $7.95 to $34.95 include prime rib, pork tenderloin casserole, fried catfish, stir-fried chicken, and butt steak, appealing to a variety of budgets and palates. In addition to large entree portions, dinners come with soup, salad, potato, vegetable, relish tray, and bread. I highly recommend the 22-ounce T-bone, but other delicious steaks are the New York sirloin, ribeye, porterhouse, shish kebab, and the Chateaubriand for two. Those in the lounge can choose from an array of sandwiches ($5.95-$9.95) or appetizers ($3.95-$7.95) such as oysters, shrimp cocktail, fried smelt, and calamari.

Open Mon. - Thurs. 11 a.m. - 11 p.m., Fri. - Sat. 11 a.m. - 12 p.m. Sun. 4 p.m. - 10 p.m.

Drop the Bomb on Me!

Fleckenstein's Bakery
19225 LaGrange Rd.
708/479-5256
Fleckinstein's is probably the most popular bakery in the area and a personal favorite. Then again, I would put my seal of approval on any establishment brilliant enough to create the mother of all birthday cakes—the decadent Atomic Layer Cake. For those unfamiliar with this pastry blast: it consists of one layer of vanilla cake, a layer of banana filling, one layer of chocolate cake, one sugary layer of strawberry filling, and yet another layer of vanilla cake all topped with either buttercream or regular frosting. Though birthday and wedding cakes are their specialty, donuts, cookies, sweet rolls, and pastries are also made fresh daily.
Open Tues. - Fri. 5 a.m. - 5:30 p.m., Sat. - Sun. 5 a.m. - 3:30 p.m. Closed Mon.

Villa Pizzeria
11006 Front St.
708/479-5055
The romantic setting of this quaint restaurant, with its dark lighting and candle-lit tables of the red and white checkered variety, would make Tom and Jerry look like Lady and the Tramp. And now that I've planted that scene in your head, just try to erase the image of two dogs kissing. (There's an appetite suppressant for you.) Pizza, fries, appetizers, and sandwiches comprise the basic menu.
Open Sun. - Thurs. 4 p.m. - 10 p.m., Fri. - Sat. 4 p.m. - 12 a.m.

Little Prices, Big Meals

Little Al's
11034 Front Street
No phone
Popular as an afterwork hangout and for its friendly, small town atmosphere, Little Al's is a dimly-lit bar/restaurant located across the street from the train station in the heart of downtown Mokena. I have yet to set foot in Little Al's when it is not busy.

You only need a little cash to get a big meal at Little Al's. As little as $16 can feed a party of four with a chicken sandwich/fries, hoagie/fries, cheeseburger/fries, combo basket (15 onion rings, 11 zucchini,

12 mushrooms), and chicken wings (about 15 with BBQ sauce). The chicken drumsticks, smothered with Open Pit, are spicy, loaded with meat, and so huge that they could provide a meal in themselves. However, the menu's highlight is the hoagie: the meat has a salty, spicy flavor that is just right, plus the sandwich comes with the perfect amount of trimmings and is served on garlic bread.

SHOPPING

The Stop Shop for the Crafty Person

Mokena Sales
Craftsville
11104 Front St.
708/479-5266
Sorry gentlemen, now there is no excuse for you not going craft shopping with the ladies. At Mokena Sales, luckily, you can putz around with the tools on the first floor, while others peruse the crafts and collectibles upstairs in "Craftsville." The concept is new, so it's not as large as other craft stores, but it will be soon. And, they do have a nice selection of Precious Moments and Beanie Babies.
Open Mon. - Fri. 9 a.m. - 7 p.m., Sat. 9 a.m. - 5 p.m. Closed Sun.

Smallest Antique Store

Farmhouse Antiques
The Jan and Lee Puig Farm
107600 W. 191st St.
708/479-7017
Don't be fooled by the size of Farmhouse Antiques. Who says you can't find great deals in a tiny, shed-like building on a farm, next to a large vegetable stand? It takes about 30 seconds to walk through the entire store, but about 30 minutes to look at all the antiques. Here you'll find antique furniture, vintage clothing, Hoover vacuums, Hollywood memorabilia, ephemera, china, and silverware. A nice, clean, well-kept store that is worth a visit!
Open Tues. & Thurs. 10 a.m. - 5 p.m. and weekends "when they're around."

Baker Interiors
11028 Front St.
708/479-2228
This quaint craft and floral shop on Mokena's Front Street holds regular tea parties and home decoration/craft demonstrations for $10-$14 per person. Such events might include chair massages, Christmas decorating advice, or a tea party accompanied by harp music.
Open Tues. - Thurs. 9 a.m. - 5 p.m., Fri. 9 a.m. - 7 p.m., and Sat. 9 a.m. - 5 p.m.

LODGING

Motel 8
9485 W. 191st
708/479-7808
Motel 8 maintains 169 rooms, including six suites with kitchens, at the bargain rates of about $45 per night on weekdays and $65 per night on weekends. Each room is equipped with AC, color TV with cable, king size beds, and double-sink bathrooms. A complimentary breakfast is served.

Mokena Ordinances

Every lot is required to have one tree per 40 feet of lot frontage.

Forget about hard water deposits on your drinking glasses. You've got bigger things to worry about—like mullers! Yes, it is unlawful for any person to throw or deposit any offal, or other offensive muller, or the carcass of any dead animal in any watercourse in Mokena.

MONEE

Just The Facts

Village of Monee
From Indians to Industry
40 miles from Chicago

Contact:
Village Hall 708/534-8301

Access via:
I-57

HISTORY

Monee was named for the half Ottawa Indian princess daughter of French fur trader Monsieur Antoinne La Fevre.

RECREATION

Will County's First Public Fishing Lake

Monee Reservoir
27341 Ridgeland Ave.
708/534-8499
Monee Reservoir offers rowboat and pedal boat rentals for $20 a day. Bringing your own rowboat or pedal boat is prohibited, however you may bring boats with electric trolling motors. Fishing poles are available for $2.50/hour or $10/day. Fishing regulations allow one Large Mouth Bass (15") and six Channel Catfish (no size limit).

If fishing bores you, try throwing some horseshoes ($10/day) in the picnic area. Rentals run $25 for a pavilion and $15 for a picnic grove. A 2.5 mile hiking trail is also accessible from the reservoir.
Summer 6 a.m. - 8 p.m., winter 8 a.m. - 5 p.m.

Fishing Clinics
Monee Reservoir
708/534-8499
Monee Reservoir offers a Beginner's Fishing Clinic each year in April that teaches students how to tie a basic knot, assemble equipment, choose bait, and cast without hooking your fishing mates. The cost is only $6 for out-of-county residents and $3 if you live in county.

ENTERTAINMENT

Over the Edge
25520 S. Governors Highway
708/534-8900
When you're hanging out with friends, all bars are pretty much the same. It's the crowd, atmosphere, and drink specials that make the difference, right? Over the Edge provides two of the three (they can't help you in the friend department) with shot specials and daily activities. There's country line dancing on Tuesdays, Ladies Nite on Thursdays, five-cent drafts on Fridays, and live music and open mic on the weekends.
Open Mon. - Fri. 3 p.m. - 2 a.m., Sat. 6 p.m. - 1 a.m.

MORRIS

RECREATION

Largest Tract of Prairie in Illinois

Goose Lake Prairie State Park
5010 N. Jugtown Rd.
815/942-2899
Not only does Goose Lake have the largest area of Prairie land in Illinois, but certain areas bear traces of native plants and remain much the way they were 150 years ago. Lake Heidecke, located nearby, provides fishing and duck hunting activities. The lake is stocked regularly: the East End is said to provide the best view. Trails near both lakes take hikers through eight-foot Indian grass and an array of different plants and flowers.
Open daily 10 a.m. - 4 p.m.

Only State Park Designated for Jet Skiing

William G. Stratton State Park
Gebhard Woods
815/942-0796
Jet skiing, boating, water skiing, and fishing are all allowed on the Illinois River at this state park, however, there is absolutely no swimming.
No fee—bring your own equipment. Open dawn - dusk.

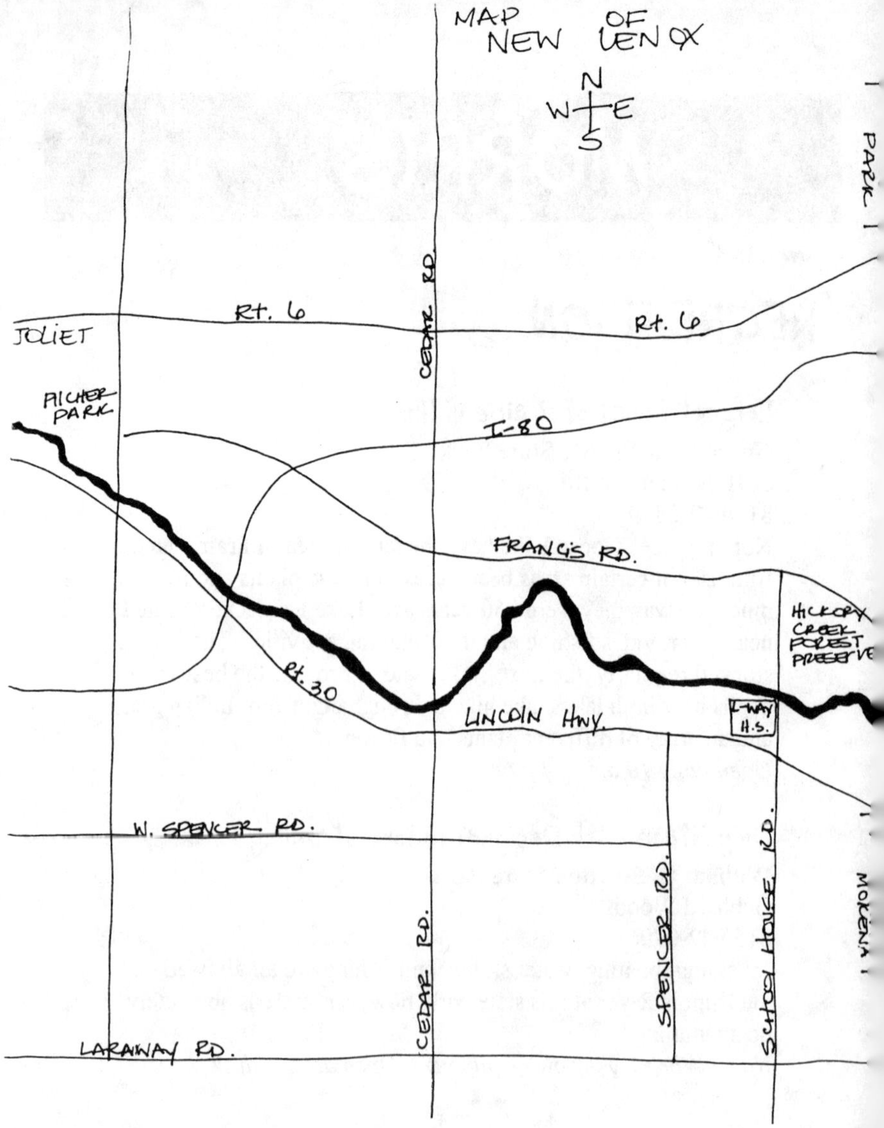
MAP OF
NEW LENOX
N
W
E
S
PARK
CEDAR RD.
Rt. 6
Rt. 6
JOLIET
PILCHER PARK
I-80
FRANCIS RD.
HICKORY CREEK FOREST PRESERVE
Rt. 30
LINCOLN HWY.
L-WAY H.S.
W. SPENCER RD.
CEDAR RD.
SPENCER RD.
SCHOOL HOUSE RD.
MOKENA
LARAWAY RD.

New Lenox

NEW LENOX

Just The Facts

Village of New Lenox
"Home of Proud Americans"
36 miles south of the Loop

Land Area	9 sq. miles
Median Age	32.5
Median income	$ 50,187
Average Sale Price of Home	$165,684

Population:

1990	6,128
1994	12,080
2010	13,636

Contacts:
Village Info Line 815/485-7700
New Lenox Village Hall 815/485-6452
http://www.lincolnnet.net/communities/newlenox/newlenox.htm (village)
http://www.lincolnnet.net/nltwp (township)

Access via:
I-80, Rt. 6, Rt. 30, I-55, and I-57

HISTORY

New Lenox, formerly Van Horne's Point, is one of the oldest settlements in northern Illinois. The French established a trading post here in 1728, but the first permanent non-Indian settlers didn't arrive until 1829. The area was incorporated in 1946 with a name given to honor the town's first supervisor who came from Lenox, New York. Thanks to the local parks, woods, and roads such as Van Horne Woods; Pilcher Park; and Francis, Haven, and Gougar roads, the names of other early settlers live on. New Lenox's activity and population growth started much earlier than other towns in the area. From reading early accounts and history, it's easy to see that this was a wealthy "party" town in the 1800s.

New Lenox is home to two high schools, Providence and Lincoln-Way, the latter of which is one of the largest high schools in Illinois and was ranked in *Money* magazine as one of the top 100 high schools in the country. The graduates of Lincoln-Way are also extremely gifted and intelligent . . . just ask any of our former teachers. Providence has its own distinction: though both schools were football state champs in 1997, it was Providence's fourth straight title.

TOURING

Van Horne's Cabin
Methodist Church Campground
Rt. 30 past Cedar

Perhaps the most prominent person in New Lenox history was C.C. Van Horne, who taught at the first school in the vicinity in 1832. He resided in a cabin which was then called Van Horne's Point, but is now the Campgrounds of the Methodist Church. This small log cabin is easily seen from Rt. 30 driving west towards Joliet.

Haven Street
Off of Rt. 30
Haven is the oldest street in New Lenox and contains houses dating to the mid-1800s. The town's first blacksmith shop as well as the first dentist's and doctor's homes are on this street. Unfortunately, the first tavern and post office have been razed to make way for new construction, but the historical society is taking steps to insure that in the future, buildings of historical significance will not be torn down.

We're #1! We're #1!

In 1899 New Lenox became the first community with rural telephones in the United States.

In the mid-1800s, resident Ormus Holmes invented a knotter which tied grain into bundles.

The first post office in Will County opened in New Lenox in 1833.

Trinity Lutheran Church
504 N. Cedar
Cedar and Elm
Trinity, although only about 48 years old, bears a limestone look comparable to some of the oldest churches in the SS.

The Sanctuary
New Lenox Park District
485 N. Manor
This beautiful, 177-acre, 18-hole championship golf course overlooks a backdrop of untouched trees and hills. The Sanctuary hosts a driving range, indoor and outdoor restaurants, and a stunning view of the 6,700-yard Scottish-links-style course. A Frank Lloyd Wright style Prairie clubhouse is the centerpiece of this dramatic setting.

Depression Cure

New Lenox was a shipping center for the Midwest's many grain, dairy, and poultry farms. It was described in *Arden Acres*, a novel of the 1930 Depression by Jessica North MacDonald, as a new and distant subdivision on the Rock Island Railroad. The book opens: "ARDEN ACRES. The great yellow billboard screamed at the passers-by. Arden Acres. Lots as low as five hundred dollars. Only fifty miles from Chicago's Loop. Start a chicken farm, a rabbit farm. Make your lot earn your living."

ENTERTAINMENT

Bogey Bogey Par Par Bogey Bogey

Doc Bogey's Golf Range
1508 S. Spencer Rd.
815/485-1899
Doc Bogey's, a ma and pa driving range "ran mostly by pa," opens for the spring and summer months. The range offers 20-plus stalls and charges $4 per bucket and $3 for a refill. Golf instruction prices vary, but fall around $15 an hour. Judy Dober, the ma portion of the partnership, states that Doc's is a family-oriented, low-pressure place to relax and have fun.

Hidden Sledding Hill
Hickory Creek Station Forest Preserve
Rt. 30
The creation of Old Plank Trail has yielded not only a great bike/ jogging path, but also some choice hills for sledding. The trail results in the "Hidden Sledding Hill" which tapers off into a flat field for safe landing. The location is currently used by only a few people, so it's not overcrowded—yet.

FOOD

Como Inn of the Burbs

Paisano's Pizza
348 W. Maple
815/485-2422
With its large booths like little rooms set off with curtains, Paisano's Old World Italian atmosphere is an instant reminder of Chicago's Como Inn. Don't order from Paisano's unless you're hungry—very hungry. The meal portions are thick and filling, so make room in your refrigerator for leftovers before leaving home. Try the veal sandwich with red sauce and mozzarella cheese on a large French roll and the pepperoni pizza bread. Paisano's is extra, super, very (insert additional superfluous adjectives here) generous with their cheese. The dairy can measure a quarter of an inch high on their

pizzas! The beef sandwich with green olives is always a unanimous winner.

Simply Sweets
336 W. Maple
815/485-8633
Calling all candy fanatics! Whatever your candy craving, I promise, you'll find a cure for that ailing sweet tooth ailment here. For gummy "whatever" freaks like me, Simply Sweets stocks every gummy, chewy creature one could hope for. Salt water taffy, malt balls, nuts, old-fashioned candies, and newer varieties are also in abundant supply. Party trays that fit up to seven different candies and custom-made gift baskets are their specialty.
Open Mon. - Fri. 6 a.m. - 7:30 p.m., Sat. 9:30 a.m. - 6 p.m., Sun. 11 a.m. - 5 p.m.

Dreamy Delite
918 Timber
815/485-1988
Dreamy Delite is the classic little hot dog stand with picnic tables out front and drive-thru service. The big draw here in the summer are the flurries and banana split ice cream treats. Daily specials are of the buy-a-hamburger-and-fries-get-a-free-drink ilk. The menu also lists pizza, subs, hot dogs, and BBQ pork.
Open Sun. - Thurs. 10:30 a.m. - 8: 30 p.m., Fri. - Sat. 10:30 a.m. - 10:30 p.m.

AJ Hot Dogs and Gyros
342 Maple Ave. (Rt. 30)
815/485-8922
AJ's offers fast carry-out service, but has plenty of booths and tables for dining on site. Fast foodies can choose from every kind of dog (chili, cheese, corn), burgers with all the trimmings, gyros, fajitas, chicken sandwiches, poor boys, rib eye sandwiches, subs, veggie burritos, seafood, salads, and side orders such as poppers, pizza puffs, and cheese sticks. Loaded with four thick tomato slices, three generous green pepper slices, shredded lettuce, cucumbers, pickles, onions, three slices of American cheese, and two slices of Swiss and smeared with their special sauce, the 12" vegetable submarine is HUGE, and the taste is even bigger.
Open Mon. - Sat. 10 a.m. - 10 p.m. and Sun. 11 a.m. - 9 p.m.

The Only Organic Mushroom Farm in Illinois

Roman and Nina Kaczynski's organic mushroom farm—the only one in Illinois—consists of five underground houses. They grow crimini, portabello, and white mushrooms, which they sell to Goodness Greeness in Chicago two to three times a week. The rest are sent around the country to restaurants, retailers, and other wholesalers. *Not open to the public.*

C.P. Meat Market
1312 N. Cedar Rd.
815/485-3629
This cousin-owned meat market specializes in sausage, pre-stuffed birds, and marinated chicken and meats. They also make hamburger patties, potato pancakes, and potato pierogi, all pre-packaged and ready to go.
Open Mon. - Thurs. & Sat. 9 a.m. - 6 p.m., Fri. 9 a.m. - 8 p.m.

Sherwood Inn
1300 North Cedar
815/485-2711
The Sherwood Inn is a small local restaurant with a cozy atmosphere and a large menu selection. Highlights include the Sherwood Super Burger (1/2 lb. steak on rye with grilled onions and melted American Cheese) with fries ($5.55); Gyros plate ($6.25); and one egg, toast, and hash browns ($2.75). Fittingly, the Sherwood Inn, which is across the street from a funeral home, bears a sign reading, "Family Dining and Spirits."
Open daily 6 a.m. - 10 p.m.

Aurelio's Pizza
320 W. Maple
815/485-8100
See description and hours under *Frankfort*, p. 58.

SHOPPING

Natural Choices Health Food
16340 N. Cedar Rd.
815/485-5572
Natural Choices specializes in health pills, oils, herbs, vitamins, health foods, grains, pastas, and health drinks, with prices that are comparable to other herb stores.
Open Mon. - Fri. 10 a.m. - 6 p.m., Sat. 10 a.m. - 4 p.m. Closed Sun.

All Aboard!

Larsen Hobby
2571 Lincoln Hwy.
815/485-1991
This small shop serves mostly collectors of toy trains and die cast collectibles, but caters to other hobbyists as well with their Barbies and model sets. Reference guides and repair parts are also for sale.
Open on the weekends (hit or miss).

Collectors Dream Store

Berry's Bargain World
2571 E. Lincoln Hwy.
815/485-6724
I love Berry's Bargain World! Sporting a warehouse look, Berry's houses rows and rows of Boyd's bears, Ty collectibles (at the best prices I've seen anywhere), Harley Davidson collectibles, Precious Moments (the Southland's largest selection), collector plates, porcelain dolls, movie memorabilia, and much more. If you're not in the area, they'll check inventory for your collectible over the phone.
Open Mon., Thurs., & Fri. 9 a.m. - 8 p.m.; Tues., Wed., & Sat. 9 a.m. - 6 p.m., Sun. 9 a.m. - 5 p.m.

Petal & Twigs

The Trinity Gift Shop
427 W. Francis Rd.
815/485-5976
This 1850s Victorian farmhouse was scheduled to be razed (no one wanted it...there's a lot of that going on in the SS!) when Trinity School purchased it to house their school and gift shop. Today its

many rooms offer a beautiful shopping experience of dried flowers, aromatic candles, teddy bears, Tiffany-style lamps, Beanie Babies, stuffed animals, musical metal sculpture, wind chimes, bird houses, and assorted stained glass items.
Open Mon. - Fri. 9 a.m. - 6 p.m. and Sat. 9 a.m. - 5 p.m.

"Hidden Gem"

The Capricorn Shop
1269 North Cedar
815/485-3236
Partners La Nora Lukanich and Judy Drew couldn't have arranged a "cuter" store, one I highly recommend and keep ranting about. Capricorn uses their stock of antique furniture to display smaller sale items, which creates a museum-like shopping atmosphere in their wide-open shop. A brief run-down of their eclectic and appealing inventory must mention the following: artwork (large and small), Victorian frames, Victorian lamps, gorgeous Victorian upholstered chairs, antiques, reproduction milk bottles, blankets, ornaments, bird houses, snow village figures, figurines, Precious Moments, Cherished Teddies, Gooseberry Patch and other Enesco figures, jewelry, can-dles, candle holders, cookbooks, cocoa, teas, coffee, muffin mixes, jams, syrups, pasta mixes, herbs and spices, cookie cutters, book-marks, books, calendars, stationery, make-your-own-gift-baskets, and more. And all for excellent prices!
Open Mon. - Fri. 10 a.m. - 6 p.m., Sat. 9 a.m. - 5 p.m., Sun. 11 a.m. - 3 p.m.

Town & Country Fashions
398 N. Cedar Rd.
815/485-3122
Town and Country Fashions sells women's business, casual, and summer clothes in sizes 6-18 and XL-XXL, as well as some baby clothes. Clothing items include beautiful silk blouses and many different styles of prom and evening gowns—from a "Grace Kelly baby blue" to the traditional short-and-black. Fabulous coats, jewelry, and scarves are also for sale to complete any new outfit. This store breaks the myth that only the mall has great clothes!
Open Mon., Wed., Thurs., & Fri. 10 a.m. - 6 p.m., Tues. 10 a.m. - 8 p.m., Sat. - Sun. 10 a.m. - 5 p.m.

Shrubbery. Get Your Shrubbery.

The Will-South Cook Soil and Water Conservation District
(Say that fast 10 times!)
815/462-3106
Every fall and spring the WSCSWCD (see above) conducts a tree, shrub, and fish sale. Trees and shrubs come in all sizes and fish (to stock those garden ponds) usually include catfish, bass, sunfish, minnows, and bluegill at wholesale prices. I've often wondered what *is* the wholesale price for a crappie these days?
Call for exact dates and more information.

The Statuary
815/485-1808
When pink flamingos just aren't enough, turn to The Statuary. Distinctive statues, planters, bird feeders, fountains, stepping stones, gargoyles, and other Gothic items are among the unique collection of yard and garden decorations available.
Open Fri. - Sun. 9 a.m. - 5 p.m.

OAK LAWN

Just The Facts

Village of Oak Lawn
15 miles south of Chicago

Median Age	39.4
Median household income	$45,871
Average Sale Price of Home	$141,588

Population:

1990	56,182
1994	56,690
2010	55,702

Contact:
Chamber of Commerce 708/424-8300

Access via:
Interstates I-80, I-90, I-94, I-294, I-55, and I-57

HISTORY

Oak Lawn was originally named "Black Oak Grove" for the region's abundant black oak trees, but changed to the current name in 1882. 27 years later, the dominantly German town was incorporated with 287 residents.

Because the land which Oak Lawn sits on was once an Indian game reserve, it didn't develop as fast as surrounding areas. While other towns already had churches, a post office, and stores, residents of Oak Lawn depended on nearby Blue Island for such things.

Ordinances

No livestock or poultry may be kept in the village.

It is illegal to keep any disabled, wrecked, or abandoned vehicles or parts thereof on your property, village streets, alleys, or parkways. (Hallelujah! It should be an ordinance to have this ordinance in every town!)

The area has come a long way since then and is now a strong community based on locally-owned boutiques, shops, and delis. The intersection of 95th and Cicero Avenue is one of the busiest shopping districts in the entire metropolitan area.

On the National Register of Historic Places

Oak Lawn School
9526 S. Cook
Built in 1906, the Cook Avenue School employed Joseph Covington, a Civil War veteran and friend of Abraham Lincoln, as its first teacher.

TOURING

St. Xavier College
3700 W. 103rd St.
St. Xavier College, founded by five Irish nuns in 1846, was originally located on Michigan Avenue in Chicago. After a 1956 fire the college relocated to Oak Lawn.

RECREATION

Parks In Oak Lawn

There are more than 300 acres of parks, recreational facilities, and open land in Oak Lawn, including a **Nature Center** (9610 E. Lake

Shore Drive) with displays such as the *Web of Life* and *Kid's Corner*.

Wolfe Wildlife Wetlands
109th St. & Laramie Ave.
708/857-2200
This 45-acre wetland preserve provides a glimpse of what the area looked like hundreds of years ago. Community residents enjoy its trails, wildlife refuge, and full schedule of nature programs.
Open daily dawn - 10 p.m

ENTERTAINMENT

Southwest Symphony Orchestra
5164 W. 95th St.
708/489-5322
The Community Pavilion seats up to 3,500 and hosts a variety of events, including an annual concert series by the Southwest Symphony Orchestra.

Coolest Bar in Oak Lawn

This one's a tie between **B.J. McMahon's** and **Reilly's Daughter**, though there are enough bars in Oak Lawn to fill a whole volume. On 95th alone a different one is visible about every 10 seconds.

B.J. McMahon's
5432 W. 95th Ave.
708/422-3111
B.J. McMahon's is a "cigar-friendly" Irish bar with a sports atmosphere. And with three electronic dartboards, five TVs (of varied degrees of largeness), a jukebox, pinball games, and video games, this bar is generous in the entertainment department. Green abounds on walls, tables, chairs, and decor. Even the toilet seats have shamrocks painted on them! This is a hidden gem for the females, since the crowd is of a mid-20s, male

Traffic Tip

The intersection of 95th and Cicero Avenue ranks as one of the busiest in Cook County. Traffic counts indicate that 191,500 vehicles pass through the intersection on any given day. Don't become a statistic. Avoid the intersection.

demographic.
Open daily 11 a.m. - 2 a.m.

Reilly's Daughter
4010 W. 111th St.
708/423-1188
Everybody knows about, and has probably visited, Reilly's Daughter. It's a staple of the young suburbanite's bar life. The spacious bar offers enough room to stand around without being squashed, adequate tables, a large bar, and a stage for live music. What makes Reilly's Daughter so popular? I don't know, but it's widely known, they bring in good bands (mostly cover bands), and they draw a good crowd.
Open daily 12 p.m. - 2 a.m.

Rusty Nail
5763 W. 95th
708/636-1293
Trendy, Rat Pack wanna-bes who would rather drink a martini than chug a beer should check out the Rusty Nail. Likewise for those of you who drink certain brands of liquor not normally carried in bars: the owner will buy whatever you want, as long as you'll be here to drink it! The bartender/owner has done a great job of creating a down-to-earth, friendly atmosphere, and over the Rusty Nail's 22-year history has become known as a "matchmaker." During late night games and for the Superbowl, the owner orders pizza for those who come to watch on the big screen TV. Sundays and Mondays are karaoke nights while Fridays and Saturdays are dancing/DJ nights.
Open daily 5 p.m. - 2 a.m.

FOOD

JR's Hot Dogs
6335 W. 95th St.
708/499-2118
Not only has it been voted as the #1 place to grab a dog in the SS, but the beef sandwich isn't too shabby either.

Lodging

Where are you most likely to see Barbara Bush in Oak Lawn? No, it's not at the Fannie May candy store, it's in the Oak Lawn Hilton. This 12-story round tower is located at the intersection of 95th and Cicero Avenue and remains a popular stopping spot for many celebrities.

Most Extensive Wine List In the Area

Ken's Guest House
9900 Southwest Hwy.
708/422-4014
Ken's recently won the "award of excellence" from *Wine Spectator* Magazine for the 5th consecutive year.

OLYMPIA FIELDS

Just The Facts

Village of Olympia Fields

Contact:
Village Hall 708/503-8000

Access via:
I-94, I-80/94, I-57, and Rt. 30

HISTORY

Olympia Fields, one of the Chicago area's finest communities, has a "country club atmosphere" with quiet winding streets, plenty of green spaces, and a variety of custom-built single family homes.

The area began to attract attention back in the 1920s and 1930s when well-to-do Chicagoans ventured into the area to play golf and enjoy the scenic beauty of the Olympia Fields Country Club. Over time, some of these folks deemed Olympia Fields fit to be their year round residences.

The Town That Testosterone Built

Olympia Fields Park District
20712 Western Ave.
708/481-7313
In the autumn of 1913, a man with a dream left the Illinois Central train station in Flossmoor, Illinois and began traveling on foot towards Olympia Fields. He wandered all day through woodlands and terrain looking for the perfect location. What was he going to build? A large farm to support his family? Or perhaps a church,

hospital, or school? No, this man had only one thing on his mind—a golf course. Around this course he envisioned more golf courses, and a village to serve a growing community of individuals interested in, you guessed it, golf.

On the third day he invited a friend to explore the location, and by night there were two enthusiasts instead of one. These men were Charles Beach, the founder of the Olympia Fields Country Club and the first president of the Village of Olympia Fields; and James P. Gardner, the second president of the future 72-hole Country Club.

The golf course the men founded grew into what is now the park district (and a village landmark), and, according to plan, the town of Olympia Fields grew up around the course.

Alonzo Stagg, famed football coach of the University of Chicago, proposed the name "Olympia" to suggest the customs and athletic skill of the Olympic Games.

ORLAND PARK

Just The Facts

Village of Orland Park
"Golf Center of the World"
35 miles from Chicago

Contact:
Village Hall 708/403-6100

HISTORY

Basically, shopping and eating are the two main reasons people travel to Orland Park. Orland Park serves as the region's shopping center, with more than five million square feet of retail space. Orland Square, an enclosed mall, is the community's central retail attraction.

Sadly, most visitors view Orland Park as merely a retail center and remain blind to the fact that this place has history to it. It didn't just drop down as a gift from the shopping gods.

The area's first settler, Henry Taylor, arrived in 1843 and was followed shortly after by Jacob and Bernard Hostert. The latter two built log cabins that stand to this day and are preserved by the Historical Society. By 1879 Orland Park, which was then Sedgewick Station, started to grow as a commercial center due to railroad access. The town's most dramatic growth spurt, however, occurred in the 1950s and 1960s.

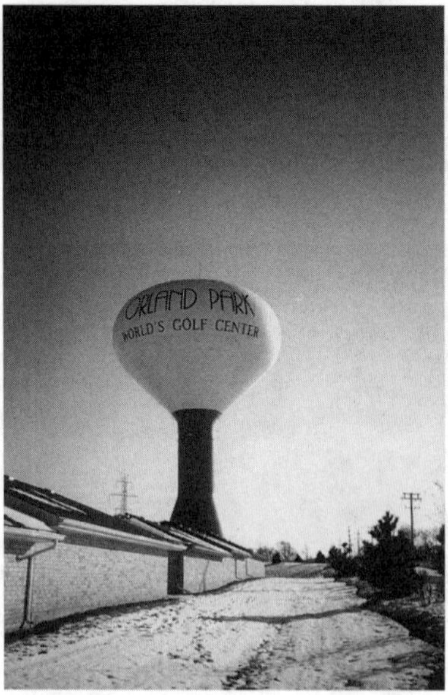

Orland Park's water tower reads "World's Golf Center" and looks remarkably like a golf ball on a tee.

TOURING

Orland Park Village Center
14750 Ravinia Ave.
I know, you're saying to yourself, "Why would I want to visit a town's village hall?" In this case, it would be to admire an award-winning design by architect Ralph Johnson of Perkins & Will that acknowledges the work of Frank Lloyd Wright. In the middle of the three village administration buildings is an outdoor amphitheater that is used for outdoor concerts.

Historical Landmarks

The Hostert Log Cabins
Near the intersection of West Avenue and 147th Street
708/349-0065 (information)
The Orland Historical Society opens the cabins to visitors on summer Sundays from 2 p.m. to 4 p.m. and by appointment. Brothers Jacob and Bernard Hostert, early settlers of the area, built these cabins prior to 1860.

On the National Register of Historic Places

Twin Towers Building
9967 144th St.
The wood-frame Twin Towers Building, built by Chicago architect William Arthur Bennett, was once the home of the Orland Park United Methodist Church, which also showed silent movies there for the town's residents. Queen Anne-style shingles contrast with the simple wood design that covers its distinct octagonal towers. This is the only

building in Orland Park on the National Register of Historic Places. Local history buffs spent nearly $200,000 to paint the building, put in new amber-frosted windows to resemble the originals, and do other touch-ups.

Town's First Post Office

Every town had them. The question is: where are they now, and what are they used for? Yes, we're talking about your town's first post office and bank. Orland Park, like many other towns, has turned theirs into antique shops.

Beacon Hill Antique Shop
14314 Beacon Ave.
708/460-7980
Open Mon. - Sat. 10:30 a.m. - 5 p.m., Sun. 12:30 p.m. - 5 p.m.
c. 1915

Original Orland State Bank

The Old Bank Antique Shop
14316 Beacon Ave.
708/460-7979
c.1910
Open Mon. - Sat. 10:30 a.m. - 5 p.m., Sun. 12:30 p.m. - 5 p.m.

Orland Park's original state bank is now an antique shop.

Humphrey House
9830 144th Pl.
Senator John Humphrey moved to the Orland area in 1846 as a child. 24 years later he entered politics and won a seat in the Illinois General Assembly in 1871 where he remained for 40 years. The Orland Park Historical Society preserves his home, which is the second oldest in the area, as a museum.
Open the second Sunday of every month from 2 p.m. - 4 p.m.

RECREATION

Bicycle Paths

John Humphrey Trail extends three miles and connects the Village Center, John Humphrey Sports Complex, Centennial Park, and the Metra Station. It's also a nice path to take if you plan on going fishing, since there are spots along the way to stop and cast.

Tinley Creek Trail is a popular Cook County Forest Preserve trail that is accessible from the parking lot at 151st Street and Catalina Drive. The 20-mile trail goes near one of the few remaining oak forests in the Chicago area.

ENTERTAINMENT

Mickadoon's Pub
8601 W. 159th St.
708/532-6707
This bowling alley/bar/restaurant provides everything you need for a fun night out. Although the menu offers many entrees, you may want to consider creating a meal out of their unique appetizers. We recommend starting with a cup of cream of potato soup seasoned withgarlic and dill, followed by an order of mini beef and bean tacos, mini corn dogs with a side of honey mustard, classic cheddar-filled jalapeño poppers and cheese garlic bread. All appetizers are less than $7, and helpings are large.
Open Tues. - Thurs. 4:30 p.m. - 10:30 p.m., Fri. - Sat. 4:30 p.m. - 10:30 p.m., Sun. 2 p.m. - 9 p.m.

FOOD

Georgios Bar and Grill, Ltd.
8888 West 159th St.
Georgios offers a nice family atmosphere and a wide range of menu items. This is really the place to go if you're in the mood for Greek Chicken. Mm, mm good! They offer dancing, all you can eat specials, daily dinner specials, daily drink specials, early bird specials, and low fat/low sodium dishes.
Open Mon. 11 a.m. - 12 a.m., bar until 1 a.m.; Tues. - Wed. & Sat. 8 a.m. - 12 a.m., bar until 3 a.m.; 11 a.m. - 12 a.m., bar until 3 a.m.

Alexi's Charhouse and Lounge
8888 W. 159th St.
708/403-9500
Sunday champagne brunch starts at 10 a.m. costs $10.95 per person. If you're a kid, senior, or football fanatic you don't want to miss Monday (kid's eat free), Wednesday (senior's discount), or Sunday and Monday (football in the lounge with free appetizers).
Open daily 10 a.m. - 11 p.m.

Continental House of Pancakes
15845 Harlem Ave.
708/429-3220
Two kinds of breakfast eaters exist: those who eat and run and those who linger with their coffee. If, on the one hand, you need to gorge and run, Continental's servers provide some of the fastest service I've seen on the SS. On the other hand, if you need a while to digest, read a paper, and gather your thoughts on world issues, Continental's servers won't nag or make you feel rushed. How about this breakfast? For a little over $5 you can dine on a skillet of hash browns topped with eggs, cheese, sausage, bacon, ham, green peppers, and onions and served with 2 large pancakes or toast and juice. They also serve lunch and dinner and have one of the most diverse salads listing I've seen (13 all together).
Open Sun. - Thurs. 6 a.m. - 9 p.m., Fri. - Sat. 6 a.m. - 10 p.m.

SHOPPING

Rated #1 of the South Suburban Malls

Orland Square Mall
151st St. & LaGrange Rd (Rt. 45)
708/349-6936
Orland Square Mall holds 150+ stores with 6,800 parking spaces. Major stores include Carson Pirie Scott, JC Penney, Marshall Field's, and Sears. Other stores include Abercrombie & Fitch, Aunt Anne's Pretzels, The Bombay Company, Eddie Bauer and Eddie Bauer Home, Kuppenheimer's, Precis, Prints Plus, Ruby Tuesday, Suncoast Motion Picture Co., TV Land, and Warner Bros. Studio Store.
Open Mon. - Fri. 10 a.m. - 9 p.m., Sat. 10 a.m. - 7 p.m., Sun. 11 a.m. - 6 p.m.

LODGING

The Essence Suites
14455 S. LaGrange Rd.
708/403-3300
Whirlpool suites range from $125 (Sunday through Thursday) to $150 (Friday and Saturday). For those who "nap" from 12 p.m. to 4 p.m. the rates decrease to $65.00. The Super Essence Suite is $165 (Sunday through Thursday) or $210 (Friday and Saturday). The Super Suite has a 186 gallon tub with a fireplace, king size waterbed, CD, VCR, TV, radio, monogrammed robes, toiletries, steam room with rain shower, mood lighting, wet bar, sink, refrigerator, microwave, coffee maker, roses, and evening snack.

PALOS HEIGHTS

Just The Facts

Palos Heights
Palos Hills
Palos Park

Access Via:
I-294, I-55, I-80, Harlem Ave., and Rte. 45

TOURING

National Landscape Award

Lake Katherine Nature Preserve
7607 W. College Dr.
708/361-1873
The Lake Katherine Preserve offers 91.3 acres of walks along the Cal-Sag area plus a waterfall, lake, arboretum, and indoor nature center. There is also a viewing area to watch the lake's duck population and birding sites along the path.
Open daily dawn - dusk.

RECREATION

Swallow Cliff Sports Area
Rt. 83 & Rt. 45
708/448-8532
I don't know what makes the dare-devils at Swallow Cliff more tired—screaming from flying down one of the largest toboggan slides in the nation or climbing up all the stairs to do it again!

Birthplace of the A-bomb

The Manhattan Project moved to the forest preserves (then the Argonne Forest) near 107th and Archer Avenue from the University of Chicago. Radioactive remains were buried in Red Gate Woods (once again-the North Side dumping on us) in the 1940s, at a site featuring two markers. One reads "The world's first nuclear reactor" and the other "Caution! Do not dig. Buried in this area is radioactive material."

Most South Suburbanites are familiar with Swallow Cliff, whether they've "been there, done that" or just driven by to admire those who can. It proudly holds the title of the highest and longest slide in the Chicago region with chutes at 400 feet long. Other amenities include an ice skating pond and ski trail.
An all-day pass costs $1 per person, Four-seater toboggans rent for $3/hour. Open daily dawn - dusk, slides open until 10 p.m. during the winter.

ENTERTAINMENT

Moraine Valley Community College
Fine & Performing Arts Center
10900 S. 88th Ave.
708/974-5500
Moraine Valley Community College serves as a primary social and cultural center for the community of Palos Hills. Its $13-million Fine and Performing Arts Center is a highlight of the campus and offers a 600-seat theater, art gallery, and meeting rooms.

FOOD

Rosewood on the Green
13248 S. 76th Ave.
708/448-0888
Rosewood on the Green, a family restaurant with a fine dining atmo-

sphere, serves up a Pasta Houlio and Linguine with Clam sauce as house specialties. Other recommended appetizers and dinners include the sausage and peppers, spaghetti and Italian meatballs, grilled portabello with mozzarella, and salmon in tarragon.
Open Sun. 3 p.m. - 10 p.m., Mon. 4 p.m. - 12 a.m., Tues. - Thurs. 11 a.m. - 12 a.m., Fri. 11 a.m. - 2 a.m.

Best BBQ Ribs

Nick's Barbecue
12658 Harlem Ave.
708/923-7427
Nick's earned a reputation in the SS for preparing some of the tastiest BBQ ribs around, so be sure to try them when visiting. You won't be disappointed. Other menu items include sandwiches (Italian beef, meatball, turkey, Philly cheesesteak, Rueben, fat boy submarine), gyros, or health conscious offerings (soup, salad, chicken). And, for fewer than ten bucks, a half slab of BBQ ribs with either chicken or shrimp is yours.
Open Sun. - Thurs. 10:30 a.m. - 10 p.m., Fri. - Sat. 10:30 a.m. - 11 p.m.

Mama Vesuvio East Restaurant
6361 College Dr.
708/371-2500
The Star readers voted Mama's the "Best Pizza on the South Side." We vote them as *one* of the best pizza joints in the South 'Burbs. An enclosed terrace patio bar is equipped with a big screen TV for sports and Friday and Saturday karaoke nights. The outdoor patio bar also has a bocce court for summer months.
Open Mon. - Sat. 3 p.m. - 2 a.m., Sun. 12 p.m. - 12 a.m.

Trivia

Palos Park was named after Palos, Spain, the city from which Columbus set sail for the New World.

William Workman murdered seven people including his mother, father, and a pregnant woman while on a shooting rampage in 1937. When police surrounded his home in Palos Hills, he came out with one hand up and one hand holding a can of beer. He was sentenced to 100-300 years.

PARK FOREST

Just The Facts

Village of Park Forest
"The Nation's First Packaged Community"

Contacts:
Village Hall 708/748-1112
http://www.lincolnnet.net/communities/parkforest/parkforest.htm

Access via:
I-57 and U.S. 30

HISTORY

In 1947, immediately after World War II, Park Forest was built as a planned community for veterans and upwardly mobile young families. The town quickly attained a national reputation for its shopping mall, industry park, educational and cultural opportunities, recreation facilities, and winding tree-lined streets.

Because of the number of professionals attracted to Park Forest after its founding, the community was studied as the basis for the 1956 classic *The Organization Man* by William Whyte.

Park Forest is home to the nationally known "Race with the String Quartet in the Woods" and the Chili's Park Forest Scenic 10-Mile Run, which is recognized as one of the "Top 100 Races in the Country" by *Runners World* magazine.

TOURING

Art Gallery of Park Forest Art Center
410 Lakewood
708/748-3377
The gallery of the Park Forest Art Center showcases the work of fine artists from throughout the country through monthly exhibits, a rotating permanent collection, and an outstanding rental and sales gallery.
Open Mon. 1 p.m. - 4 p.m. & 7:30 p.m. - 9 p.m.; Tues., Thurs., Fri., & Sat 10 a.m. - 4 p.m.; Wed. 7:30 p.m. - 9 p.m.

ENTERTAINMENT

1992 Illinois Orchestra of the Year

Illinois Philharmonic Orchestra
210 Illinois St.
708/481-7774
This award-winning orchestra is the Southland's only professional symphony orchestra. Maestro Carmon DeLeon directs the group's many beautiful chamber, pops, and other orchestral programs at various locations throughout the South Suburban region.
Prices range from $16-$28.

Illinois Theatre Center
400 N. Lakewood Blvd.
The Illinois Theatre Center brings musicals, drama, comedy, and children's theater to the community year round. Its Nathan Manilow Theatre accommodates 330 people and is equipped with a professional sound system, complete theatrical lighting, a 12-foot electrically powered drop screen on stage, acoustical backdrop, and an enclosed, raised projection booth. The summer 1999 show is *View From a Bridge.*
Tickets range from $4-$14.

The Nathan Manilow Sculpture Park
Located on the campus of Governors State University, this 22-piece collection contains monumental works by many of this century's

most important sculptors, including DiSuvero, Hunt, and Puryear, making it one of only three monumental sculpture parks in the nation. Guided tours are offered by appointment from April through October, and an audio-visual presentation is offered in the event of bad weather.
Self-guided tours are free.

An installment in Park Forest's Nathan Manilow Sculpture Park.

FOOD

Max's Red Hots
1307 Hamilton Ave.
708/534-7590
Max's Red Hots offers the standard hot dog stand varieties: a two dog special, chili dogs, cheese dogs, and chili-cheese dogs; all start at $1.50 and come with fries. They also have compatible sandwiches such as the Maxwell Street Polish, Italian Sausage, beefs, and meatballs, with nachos, cheese fries, chili-cheese fries, and mozzarella sticks on the side.
Open Sun. - Fri. 11 a.m. - 9 p.m., Sat. 11 a.m. - 6 p.m.

SPECIAL EVENTS

Annual Running of the Scenic Ten Mile Run and 5K
Labor Day
708/748-2005 (Recreation & Parks)
This nationally known race starts at 8 a.m. from downtown Park Forest. Proceeds benefit the Starlight Foundation, an organization which grants wishes and provides entertainment for seriously ill children.

The Annual Park Forest Art Fair
September
Downtown Park Forest
Orchard and Lakewood Blvd.
708/748-3377 (Park Forest Art Center)
This art fair is one of the oldest, most prestigious juried art fairs in the Chicago metro area. Over 150 artists from all over the U.S. exhibit handmade glass, ceramics, jewelry, paintings, and sculptures. *Admission and parking are free.*

PEOTONE

Just The Facts

Village of Peotone
40 miles south of Chicago

Contact:
Village Hall 708/258-3279
http://www.lincolnnet.net/communities/peotone/peotone.htm

Access Via:
Hwy. 50, I-57

HISTORY

In 1849 Daniel Booth and James Allen were the first non-Indians to set foot in Peotone, but their contemporaries Samuel Godspeed, Ralph Crawford, and James and John Cowing were the village's first permanent settlers. Legend reports that the town was named for an Indian Chief who once roamed the region. Another story claims a railroad official created names for the many stations along the Illinois & Central Railroad by using the complex procedure of combing consonants and vowels. All in all, it translates to "a good place to live in."

For most people in the region, the name Peotone probably rings a bell because of the amount of publicity it has received as the proposed site for the upcoming third major airport for the Chicago area.

Many people say that by traveling south of Frankfort you enter the Illinois Heartland. It's easy enough to drive through Peotone without

We're #1! We're #1!

A home from Peotone was featured in the 1993 Smithsonian Institute Spotlight on American Life in the late 1800s entitled, "Land of Promise, America in the 19th Century." The house featured in this exhibit was owned by Patrick Murray and was known as the "Cowing House" after the original family. It typifies the balloon-frame construction that originated in Chicago in 1830 and revolutionized home building in America. It is a two-story Greek revival built around 1885.

even realizing that this beautiful town exists. (According to legend, Al Capone knew it did and came here as a weekend retreat during Prohibition.) Walking through Peotone, one may feel as if they have been transported back in time to the late 1800s and early 1900s. The main street is lined with old buildings housing modern businesses; fortunately, Peotone's commercial areas have not given way to the modern one-stop strip malls. Residents can still go to the old-fashioned hardware store or stop in at the butcher shop. In fact, no matter where you go, Peotone radiates a relaxed atmosphere. With a little luck, the airport will not destroy this friendly farm town and its many charms.

TOURING

Peotone Cemetery
Coming Rd., one mile east of Rt. 50
708/258-6337
This, Peotone's first cemetery, was established in 1867.

Will County Fairgrounds
710 West St.
708/258-6592
Founded in 1856 by David Goodwille, the Will County Fairgrounds is the site of the annual Will County Fair. The annual August fair attracts farmers and residents from throughout the county. During the rest of the year the grounds are home to a variety of swap meets, antique sales, weddings, and parties.

H.A. Rathje Mill
Coming Rd.
In 1872 H.A. Hathju brought mill-wrights from Holland to construct the mill for the purpose of grinding wheat and rye into flour.

Peotone Public Library
Peotone Historical Museum
213 W. North St.
708/258-3436
Formerly the First Evangelical United Brethren Church, this 1899 Gothic Revival style building has been wonderfully restored. Go inside for a stunning look at the beautiful dark wood paneling and the brown, yellow, and beige Gothic stained glass windows.

104 Second St. (private residence)
This home's exterior of metal pressed to imitate limestone is characteristic of the 1890s; its existence so far north in Illinois is rare.

117 E. Crawford St. (private residence)
c. 1860
The second house built in Peotone, this clapboard cottage is the oldest surviving building in town.

FOOD

The Eagle's Nest
514 S. Governor's Hwy.
708/258-6266
The Eagle's Nest is possibly the friendliest restaurant on the face of the earth. In addition to having attentive servers and comfortable, adequate seating, this pleasant eatery serves the signature "Eagle's Nest." The huge sandwich combines tasty, generous slices of roast beef sirloin and plenty of melted American cheese on a French roll and is served with au jus, fries, and a cup of soup ($5.15). Among the 38 sandwiches ($3.25-$5.55) are the memorable pizza burger, olive burger, and turkey and Swiss croissant; dinner options include steak, veal, and ravioli.
Sandwiches $3.25-$5.15, salads $3.95-$5.55, dinners $5.25-$10.95.
Open Sun. - Thurs. 5 a.m. - 10 p.m., Fri. - Sat. 5 a.m. - 11 p.m.

Edwin's Tavern
31851 S. Rt. 50
708/258-3393
Legend maintains that this was Al Capone's "place" in Peotone. Built in 1929 during Prohibition, it was a very elaborate building for such a small town. In its original configuration as the speakeasy Miami Gardens (supposedly so named because of Capone's love for Miami vacations), Edwin's was composed of velvet-curtained booths, a dance hall, bordello, eleven upscale bedrooms, an underground garage, and maybe even a secret underground passageway. It is said that Babe Ruth, Eddie Arcarro, and Cubs manager Charlie Grimm also paid this speakeasy a visit during Prohibition. Today Edwin's is a friendly place to sit down, have a drink, and listen to the legends of Chicago's famous "Scarface." But don't just come for the history: the tavern now features pool tables, shoe pits, and the old hall for rent.
Open Mon. - Thurs. 7 a.m. - 10 p.m., Fri. - Sat. 7 a.m. - 2 a.m., Sun. 10 a.m. - 10 p.m.

Tony's Pizza
422 Governors Highway
708/258-3355
Tony's offers great, family-sized pizza at a reasonable price ($13.50). Whether you dine in or carry out, all of their food is YUMMY! Not only do they serve pizza, but they create excellent beef sandwiches, baked mostaccioli, chicken or veal Parmesan, shrimp manicotti, and much more.
Open Mon. - Thurs. 11 a.m. - 10 p.m., Fri. - Sat. 11 a.m. - 11 p.m., Sun. 12 p.m. - 10 p.m.

Fuccio's
110 N. Second St.
708/258-6855
Lots of cheese and great sauce makes Fuccio's one heck of a pizza! A personal favorite is the pepperoni. They also serve a tasty appetizer called Tacoquitoa which is taco meat rolled up into bite size taco shells dipped in salsa—mm, mm good! They also serve a wide variety of Italian dishes as well as sandwiches.

SHOPPING

Johnson's Greenhouse
447 S. Governors Highway
708/258-3244
If you like flowers and knick-knacks, you'll love Johnson's. They always seem to offer a great deal on floral arrangements, decorations, ceramics, and florals from the greenhouse—not to mention Beanie Babies.
Open Mon. - Sat. 8:30 a.m. - 5 p.m.

SOUTH HOLLAND

Just The Facts

Village of South Holland
"Village of Churches"
23 miles south of Chicago

Contact:
Village Hall 708/210-2900

Access Via:
I-80, I-90, and I-94

TOURING

Midwest Carvers Museum
16236 Vincennes Ave.
708/331-6011
Can you imagine the amount of patience it would take to chisel a cowboy charicature down to the finest detail out of wood? OK, maybe you don't have the time to carve one for yourself, but at least you can see such works by local and internationally known artists on display at the Midwest Carvers Museums. Revolving exhibits feature some 800 stunning carvings done by members.
Donations appreciated, but not required. Open Mon. - Sat. 10 a.m. - 4 p.m.

So...

The South Holland area was the setting for Edna Ferber's novel *So Big* (1924).

RECREATION

Sand Ridge Nature Center
15890 Paxton Ave.
708/868-0606
Operated by the Forest Preserve District of Cook County, Sand Ridge concentrates heavily on the local history of the Calumet area. Events include leaf and tree identification, Native American awareness, bird walks, fall color walks, fireside chats, bat workshops, examining the skulls of prairie animals, night hikes, film fests, and winter walks.
Open Mon. - Sun. 9 a.m. - 4 p.m.

We're #1! We're #1!

The growing of onion sets became the focus of South Holland's farmers prior to World War II. By the 1940s, they claimed the title, "Onion Set Capital of the World," due to their annual production of more than 1.5 billion onion sets annually.

STEGER

Just The Facts

Steger
35 miles south of Chicago

Access via:
Hwy. 1, Rt. 30, and I-57

HISTORY

Steger is the creation of John Valentine Steger who moved his piano factory and many of its workers to the area. In the 1920s, Steger was the world's largest manufacturer of pianos.

In 1871 at the age of 17 with 12 cents in his pocket, John Steger arrived in New York from Germany, speaking no English. He repaired icehouses on the Hudson River to make money to start his own business and move westward. He married Louise Jacobs, daughter of one of Chicago's earliest settlers in 1873. His own manufacturing methods for the pianoforte evolved during his study of the instrument.

After owning several locations in Chicago, Steger bought 20 acres and moved to what is now Steger. He moved to 35th and Chicago Road after acquiring Smith & Nixon, a competitor at that location. At its peak, Steger employed 3,500, made 100 pianos a day, and produced 30,000 phonographs a year.

Steger's factory long ago faded from the scene, but the village's unique industrial tradition continues. Today, a spaghetti-maker is the village's largest employer.

Thornton

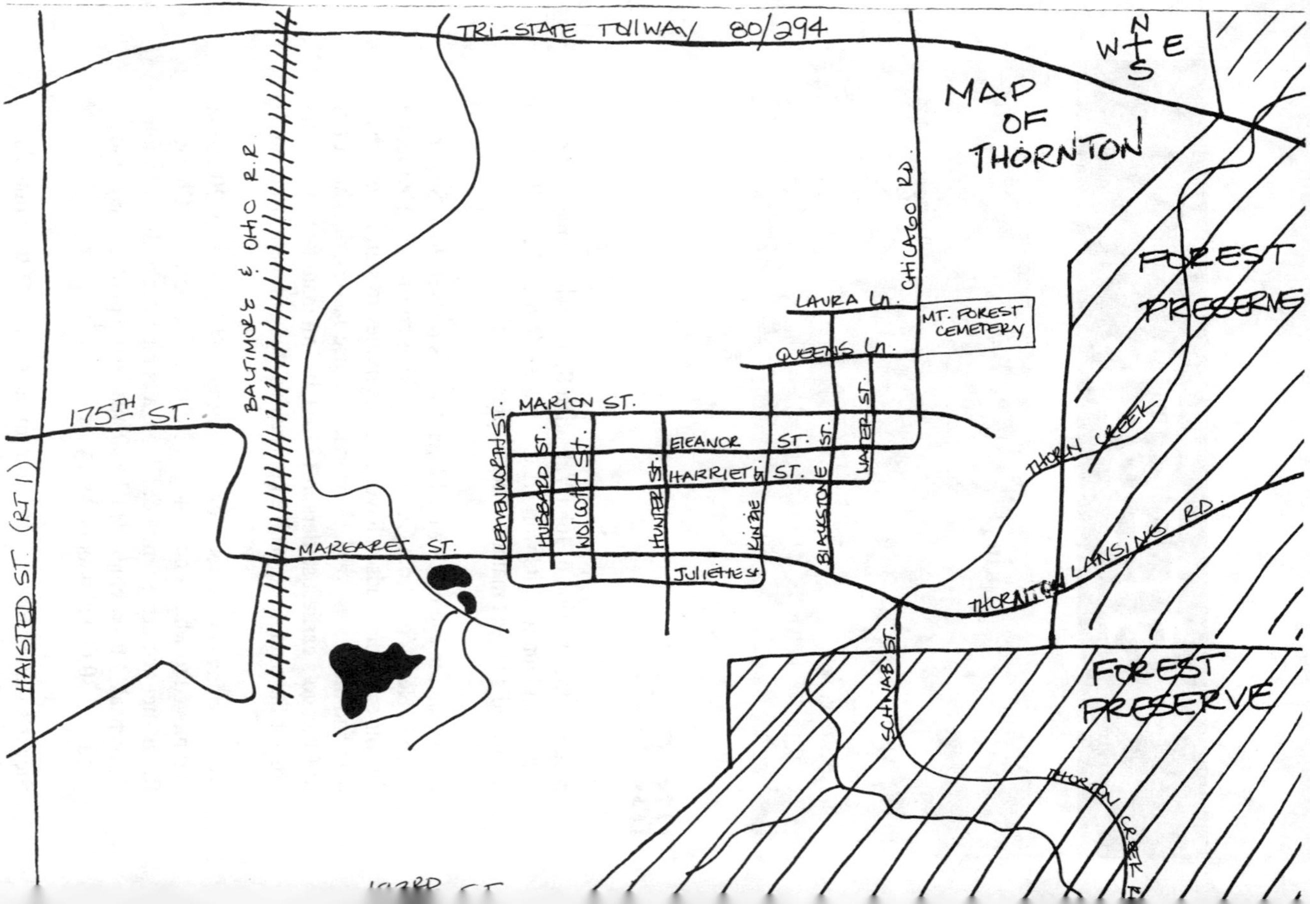

MAP OF THORNTON
N
W
E
S
TRI-STATE TOLLWAY 80/294
BALTIMORE & OHIO R.R.
175TH ST.
HALSTED ST. (RT 1)
MARGARET ST.
LEAVENWORTH ST.
MARION ST.
HUBBARD ST.
WOLCOTT ST.
HUNTER ST.
ELEANOR ST.
HARRIET ST.
KINBE
BLACKSTONE
WATER ST.
JULIETTE ST.
LAURA LN.
QUEENS LN.
CHICAGO RD.
MT. FOREST CEMETERY
FOREST PRESERVE
THORN CREEK
THORNTON LANSING RD.
SCHNAB ST.
FOREST PRESERVE
THORTON CREEK

THORNTON

Just The Facts

Village of Thornton
"Largest Commercial Quarry in America"
25 miles from Chicago

Land Area	2.3 sq. miles
Median Age	35.8
Median Family Income	$44,464

Population:

1990	2,778
1994	2,772
2010	2,902

Contact:
Village Hall 708/877-4456

Access via:
Ridge Rd. off of Halsted (Rt. 1), the tri-state tollway, and U.S. 6

HISTORY

In 1834 William Woodridge settled along the east bank of Thorn Creek (then Hickory Creek). The following year he built the first store in the village and sold his farmland to Kinzie, Blackstone, and Hubbard. Kinzie, the first mayor of Chicago, platted the village in 1835 and named it in honor of Colonel W.F. Thornton, one of the first canal commissioners in Illinois.

Kinzie, Blackstone, and Hubbard saw the same potential in Thornton that they saw in Chicago. The waterway, quarry, location, and the Chicago & Eastern Illinois Railroad destined Thornton to be the next metropolis, or so they forecasted. Thornton never became the next Chicago, however, but remained a small bedroom community.

Driving into Thornton is like slowly driving back in time. The unreadable old graves lining Thornton Cemetery will take you back to the 1800s. Shortly after passing the cemetery you'll come to an intersection of false building fronts—the town's first business, tavern, and residence.

While Thornton is not blessed with abundant restaurants, retail stores, or nightspots, it possesses more recreation and architectural touring opportunities than many towns.

TOURING

Thornton Quarry
"The Grand Canyon of the South Suburbs"
708/877-6540
Est. 1836
Millions of years ago, an inland sea covered the Midwest, which sat atop a coral reef. The Thornton quarry contains some of the most famous 410-million-year-old reefs in the Chicago area. Fossils can be readily found on a trip through the quarry.

A diameter of approximately one mile and marketable stone going to a depth of 400 feet make Thornton Quarry the largest commercial limestone quarry in the country. Nine million tons of rock are mined out of the quarry each year and made into thirty-six different products—from large boulders to stone sand. The quarry has been owned and operated by Material Services Corporation since 1938.

Thorn Creek

Thorn Creek, amazingly, was at one time 40-feet wide with a low depth of six feet. It served as a main waterway for trappers who traveled between St. Louis and Mackinac Island. Thorn Creek Woods Nature Preserve consists of 500 acres of prairies, marshes, and forest preserves.

Site of First Tavern

Corner of Williams and Margaret St.

c. 1836

Don Carlos Berry, one of the first men to enter the Northwest Territory, built the town's original tavern in 1836. He was also the

We're #1! We're #1! Or Are We?

Thornton was one of the first settled areas in Cook County. In fact, some history books tell conflicting stories as to which settled first: Thornton or Chicago. According to the book "History of the Village" from the Historical Section of the State Library in Springfield, Thornton is the oldest in Cook County.

Thornton dates back to the 1830s, when it became the site of what was once the world's largest commercial limestone quarry. The quarry is still in operation, and the foundations of many area homes are made of limestone taken from the town's very own 410-million-year-old fossil reef.

Prehistoric relics were discovered by Ira Gardner in 1871 in the area now known as Wampum Lake Forest Preserve.

The Thornton quarry is still the largest commercial limestone quarry in America, and the second largest in the world. In 1994, a 4.6 billion-year-old meteorite was discovered in the quarry.

first postmaster.

First Home in Thornton
214 Margaret St. (between Eleana St. and Harriet St.)
c. 1834
The oldest building in Thornton was once its first general store, an inn, and the former home of John Kinzie.

Historic Markers of Thornton
115 S. Kinzie Street
Only historic markers remain of the home of John Stolzenbach (c. 1877) that would later be the residence of Chicago's first and future mayor, John Kinzie.

Prisoner of War Camp
During World War II, some 350 German prisoners of war were housed in an old civilian conservation corps camp built during the Depression, in the woods near Thornton.

They picked onions and tomatoes, canned fruits, and shoveled fertilizer both at the camp and for local farmers who paid pennies a day for their labor. Remaining buildings have since been demolished and the area is now used as a family picnic area.

FOOD

Widow McCleary's Pub & Grill
400 Margaret
708/877-1234
Margaret Mary McCleary and her husband Sean Patrick purchased this building around the turn of the century when it was a brewery. Local lore has it that Al Capone visited the McClearys during Prohibition and "suggested" a business partnership. After the husband's refusal a fire destroyed the brewery, and Sean Patrick disappeared. Shortly afterward, the widow gave in to Capone. and then she too disappeared and was never heard from again. While the building was undergoing renovation in 1950, ten bodies were found. Rumor assigns one set of bones to Sean McCleary.

Today the building houses a casual pub appropriately named Widow McCleary's that offers a wide variety of menu items from mini tacos, nachos, chicken strips, chicken wings, baked clams, and poppers as appetizers to entrees of barbecue ribs, fried chicken, pork chops, steak, king crab, and fish; and six chicken sandwiches, eight burgers, club sandwiches, Italian beef, and cheesesteaks for lighter meals. *Appetizers $2-$6.95, sandwiches $3.25-$6, and entrees $4.50-$18.75. Open Tues. - Thurs. 11:30 a.m. - 1 a.m., Fri. 11:30 a.m. - 2 a.m., Sat. 3 p.m. - 2 a.m., Sun. 3 p.m. - 1 a.m. Closed Mon.*

Real Estate Agents From Hell: Joe and Kate Benders

Accounts state that in the early 1800s Kate and Joe Bender kept a hotel on Thornton Road with a sign in the window announcing land for sale at 50 cents an acre. Unknowing victims would scrape up all their money and enter the hotel only to be politely seated on a trap door that Kate would spring. The stunned victim fell to the basement and met their death with Joe Bender and his hammer. In those days, families sold off their wagons, horses, linens, and other belongings in big cities for money, so it was not suspicious when Joe Bender sold victims' goods in Chicago and Indiana. The deception and murders continued for six or seven years until neighbors finally got wind that something suspicious was going on. Turned out the ol' Benders buried victims in over 40 acres of their land. These were some of the most gruesome mass murders in the Old West—and it happened right here in Thornton.

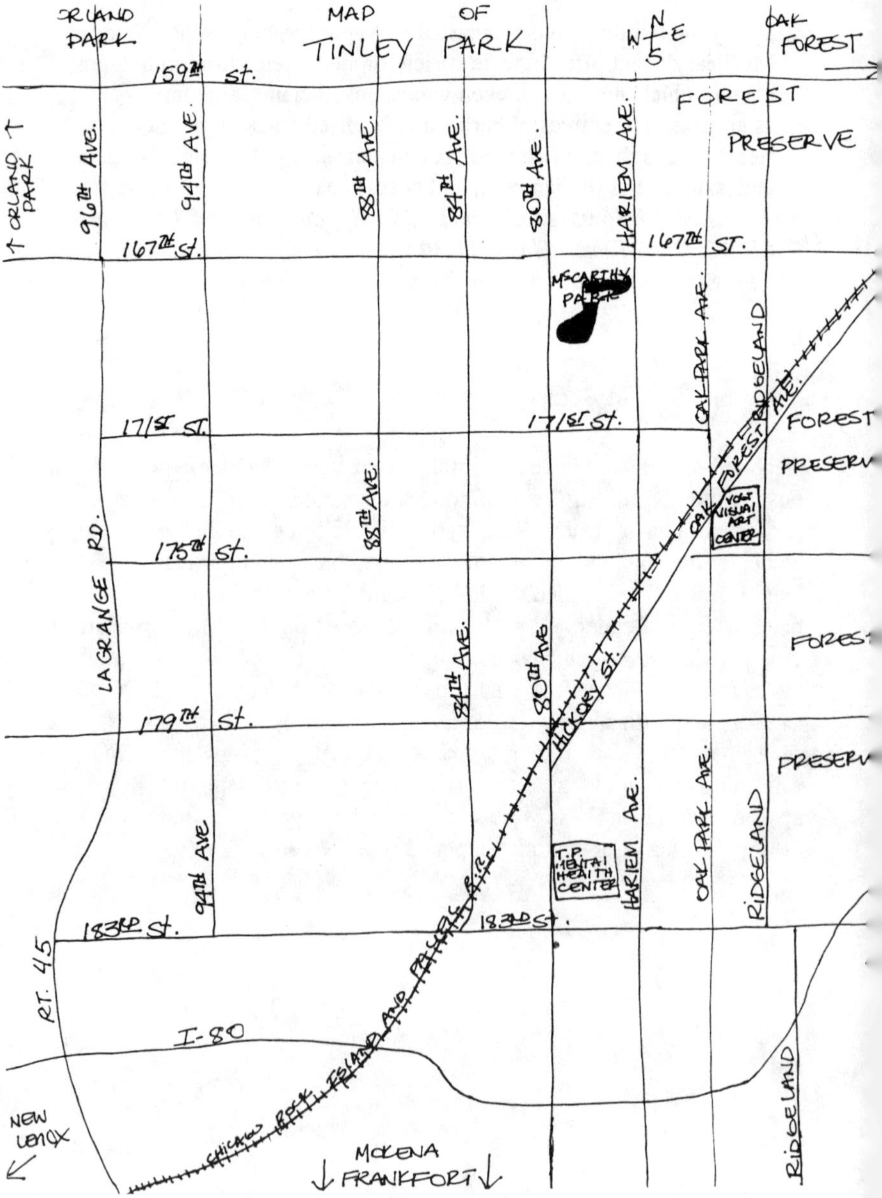
MAP OF TINLEY PARK
ORLAND PARK
OAK FOREST
N
S
E
W
159TH ST.
167TH ST.
171ST ST.
175TH ST.
179TH ST.
183RD ST.
96TH AVE.
94TH AVE.
88TH AVE.
84TH AVE.
80TH AVE.
HARLEM AVE.
OAK PARK AVE.
RIDGELAND
OAK FOREST AVE.
HICKORY ST.
LAGRANGE RD.
RT. 45
I-80
FOREST PRESERVE
McCARTHY PARK
VOGT VISUAL ART CENTER
T.P. MENTAL HEALTH CENTER
CHICAGO ROCK ISLAND AND PACIFIC R.R.
NEW LENOX
MOKENA
FRANKFORT
ORLAND PARK

Tinley Park

TINLEY PARK

Just The Facts

Village of Tinley Park
"A World Class Community"
29 miles south of Chicago

Land Area	14.0 sq. miles
Median Age	31.8
Median Family Income	$49,105
Average Sale Price of Home	$161,185

Population:

1990	37,115
1994	41,092
2010	44,064

Contacts:
Village Hall 708/532-7700
http://www.ECNet.Net/users/gtinpark/

Access via:
I-80 and I-57, Rt. 30, and Harlem Ave.

HISTORY

Originally called New Bremen, Tinley Park was re-named after its first railroad agent, Samuel Tinley, Sr. Permanent settlement began in the 1830s (the same year Chicago was planned at the site of Fort Dearborn) and was officially established in 1853. It's evident that the early pioneers, having erected the first indoor running water system and electric utility in Tinley Park, were men of vision who saw a prosperous future for their town.

Today, this booming young town (yes, it's still expanding) bears many personalities and appears to be made up of various little neighborhoods. In downtown Tinley Park, Oak Park Avenue and historic buildings along it are the focus for future restoration; Bogart's and Gambone's remain its focal points. Harlem and 159th, a busy shopping district, is home to businesses such as Wal-mart, Super K, major grocery chains, Sam's, and various shopping plazas. Another face of Tinley Park is 80th Avenue, a young booming area filled with commuters who can be seen (and laughed at) daily running to their cars and racing like maniacs out of the parking lot. 80th Avenue is usually the stop seen on the TV news during the "commuter safety" segments informing viewers how not to run in front of trains.

Tinley Park's greatest fame came when five Indianapolis 500 race car drivers, Melvin "Tony" Bettenhausen, his sons, and cousins, moved to the area.

TOURING

In 1929 during the Great Depression, a Tinley Park real estate developer devised a way to stay afloat and help others by offering free chickens to anyone who bought one of his homes. The homeowner would then sell back chickens and eggs to help pay off the mortgage. A drive down older streets such as Highland reveals an over abundance of old, decaying chicken shacks—persisting evidence of this arrangement.

17631 Highland
Note the old smokehouse still in back of this 150-year-old residence.

Party of Five

Well, it was really nine, and it was no party. A family of young children lost their second parent and did all they could to continue working the farm and stay together. The Depression didn't help the matter, so to survive they housed a still in their barn, allegedly used by Babe Tuffanelli, a supposed bootlegger from Blue Island. Another local tells stories of the Depression in which her mother rented out the family shed to Tuffanelli for sugar storage. Two of the sisters that grew up in this home, Dolly and Molly, were the "Ranch Girls" and sang on the radio and as back-up for Gene Autry when he came to town.

Henry Vogt House
17420 S. 67th Ct.
c: 1905
Cash Store
c: 1896
Now the Vogt Visual Art Center (see p. 204), this historic building was home to a prominent early resident of Tinley Park, John Henry Vogt. Vogt owned the first "Super Mart," which carried everything from meat and dry goods to clothes and cook wear. He also owned Saenger Hall, which burned down in the 1960s and was previously the place where townspeople gathered. Mr. Vogt acquired many acres of land, some of which he rented out to farmers and some of which he donated for the Zion Lutheran Church and cemetery.

A large green veranda surrounds the Victorian Vogt house and leads to an antique stained glass door. Other notable features are the brick tower in the rear of the house that was once the kitchen and high wooden rafters on which sat a large tank that held the town's first running water system.

The home of Tinley Park super-resident John Henry Vogt is now the Vogt Visual Arts Center, a unique treasure that exposes South Suburbanites to an array of art mediums.

Why Do I Always Get the Hand-me-downs?

Carl Vogt Building
6811 Hickory St.
Carl, older brother of John and also an entrepreneur, sold John Henry the aforementioned Vogt House and built himself this red brick mansion that resembles a grand hotel and is listed on the National Register of Historic Places. Across from the train station, the home can be seen from all passing trains.

The grand Carl Vogt home is visible from trains passing through Tinley Park.

Old Zion Landmark
Tinley Park Historical Museum
6427 W. 174th St.
708/429-4210
The "Old Zion" Landmark Church—a modest, but prominent structure in the historic district—houses the Tinley Park Historical Museum.
Donations for admission appreciated. Open Wed. 10 a.m. - 2 p.m.

RECREATION

Tinley Creek Trail
708/261-8400
A system of trails winds through The Tinley Creek Forest Preserve and extends through Southwestern Cook County for eighteen miles. The path is used by walkers, roller bladers, joggers, cyclists, hikers,

and horseback riders.

Forest View Farms
5300 W. 167th
708/560-0306
Forest View Farms offers guided horseback rides through the forest preserve; a petting farm; pony rides; horse drawn hay rides; and carriage, wagon, and sleigh rides year round. This is a great place for beginning equestrians, because the guides have extra patience and take time to show riders how to direct the horse.

Be sure to take advantage of the vast forest preserves clustered along the farm's eastern and western boundaries. Trails for hiking, riding, and cross country skiing; nature walks; fishing holes and ponds; picnic sites; nearby golf courses; and other amenities are available for all to enjoy.
Horseback riding $12/hour weekdays, $13/hour weekends and holidays, plus $2 for a Cook County trail license. Helmet rental $1. Rides start around 8:30 a.m. and end one hour before dark. Children must be 9 years old and tall enough to reach the stirrups. Anyone under 18 must have a permission slip signed by their parents to ride.

Best Place to Bring the Family

Odyssey Fun World
19111 S. Oak Park Ave.
708/429-3800
Odyssey Fun World has been described as a "Vegas for Kids," only it's a little cheaper and less smoky. This is 15 acres of games, food, virtual reality videos, go-karts (two tracks), bumper boats, hydro races, and an adventure park. If you're really an arcade junkie, you'll be interested to know that many game manufacturers test their games at this Fun World before distributing them on a larger scale.
No general admission fee: pay as you play. Tokens run 25 cents each or $5/20, $10/45, and $20/95. Exploration adventure $5.75 ages 4-12, $3.74 ages 1-3, those under 1 are free accompanied by a paying child. Glacier trek $6/person. Open Sun. - Thurs. 10 a.m. - 10 p.m., Fri. - Sat. 10 a.m. - 12 a.m.

Odyssey Golf Club & Banquets
19110 S. Ridgeland Ave.
708/429-7400
One of the Southland's most beautiful and challenging golf courses, Odyssey was designed by two-time U.S. Open Champion, Curtis Strange. If you're looking for a location for a reception or large party, the club's banquet hall is elegant and beautiful with its lovely balconies and large glass doors. Also as an aside to golf...I hate to give away this secret, but if you are in search of a buffet with great food and a reasonable price that's not crowded, it's here: weekend brunches include crepes, eggs, sausage, bacon, chicken, beef, fresh fruit and cheeses, champagne, orange juice, and more.
Golf rates run from $33 on weekdays to $60 on the weekends. Brunch prices are $13.55/adults, $7.55/ children. Open for brunch Sun. 10:30 a.m. - 2:30 p.m.

ENTERTAINMENT

Hidden Gem of the South Suburbs

Vogt Visual Art Center
Housed in the Henry Vogt House (see p. 201)
17420 S. 67th Ct.
708/614-6503
The Vogt Visual Art Center is a unique treasure in the SS, a center where the community can admire and be exposed to art of all mediums. The first floor is a bright, spacious gallery which displays different types of art from stained glass to wooden decoys. Past exhibitors have included John Ruthven, a famous international artist whose work has been commissioned by presidents, and John Whitney, who creates woodcarvings that need to be touched to verify they're really wood! This award winning art gallery exhibits pieces on consignment and supports themselves with commissions on sales, class fees, workshops, senior projects, daycamps, and studio rental ($2.50/hr). They also sponsor chamber music concerts (*Peter and the Wolf* was one noteworthy production) and high tea.
The gallery is open free of charge to the public; concert tickets run $6-$8. Memberships are $30 for families and $15 for senior citizens. Open Mon. 4:30 p.m. - 7 p.m., Tues. & Thurs. 1 p.m. - 7 p.m., Wed. & Fr. 1 p.m. - 4 p.m., and Sat. 10 a.m. - 4 p.m.

Mosh, Drink, and Be Merry

New World Music Theatre
Ridgeland Ave. & Flossmoor Rd.
708/614-1616
Dubbed the nation's largest outdoor pavilion, the New World Music Theater has a capacity to hold 27,000 and lures conert-goers from all over Chicagoland and beyond.
Open May - Sept.

FOOD

Aurelio's Pizza
708/429-4600
See *Frankfort*, p. 58 for hours and description.

New China Buffet
16141 S. Harlem Ave.
708/802-5288
New China Buffet offers an excellent buffet, with items such as pork egg rolls, Crab Rangoon, chicken, onion rings, egg foo young, sweet biscuits, egg rolls, egg drop soup, and fried green beans spread over three tables. It's also reasonably priced: the luncheon buffet costs $5.49 and dinner and Sunday buffets cost $7.29.
Open Sun. - Thurs. 11 a.m. - 9 p.m., Fri. - Sat. 11 a.m. - 10 p.m.

Cozy Corner Restaurant
15917 S. Harlem
708/429-4111
Cozy Corner is a great place to go late at night if you're looking for an evening snack and aren't really concerned about quick service. The menu lists breakfasts (omelettes, eggs, pancakes, and waffles starting under $1!); lunches (try the patty melt or turkey club); and dinners (the beef tips with grilled onions is a favorite at $8.95).
Open daily 6 a.m. - 11:50 p.m.

Golf 'n' Dogs
16532 Oak Park Ave.
708/633-7888
Golf 'n' Dogs mirrors the classic 1950s drive-ins which have become

pretty popular with the Baby Boomers. I recommend the basic hot dog served with all the fixings and fries. If not, there's also chicken, Italian beef, sausage, burgers, and patty melts.
Miniature golf runs $3.50 for adults and $2.50 for children. Open Sun. - Thurs. 9 a.m. - 8 p.m., Fri. - Sat. 11 a.m. - 11 p.m. Food served 11 a.m. - 10 p.m.

Best Sport's Bar in Tinley Park

Gambone's
179th & Oak Park Ave.
708/429-4949
Hidy Ho! Gambone's boasts one of the friendliest atmospheres in the SS. One portion of the restaurant is filled with large, comfortable booths; the other is the bar room with ceiling-to-floor windows. You would never expect this little gray corner building to be the best sports bar in Tinley Park, but it is.

The lunch menu includes lemon-peppered chicken breast ($6.95), Cajun steak sandwich ($7.95), three-cheese burger ($7.50), and my favorite, turkey and Swiss ($5.75). Seven other lunches are available for under $4. For dinner try one of the thin, double decker, stuffed, or taco pizzas and sample from the large selection of appetizers, including the excellent quesadillas. Other specialties for which they are famous are the panzerotti (similar to a rolled up pizza) and the Chicken à la Mamma Gambone—a tender piece of chicken in white wine sauce with peppers and rice. Then there are the daily specials: Every Monday get a free pitcher of beer or pop with a large pizza order; Tuesday any two sandwiches are $10; Wednesday is all-you-can-eat spaghetti ($4.95) and all-you-can-sing karaoke night; and every Sunday kids eat free. Plus, bottled beers are $1.50 apiece during Bulls' games.

Fifty domestic and imported beers are available to wet your palate while you watch TV on one of the three screens in the bar area. In summer, Gambone's has a charming outdoor cafe that seats plenty.
Open Mon. - Thurs. 11 a.m. - 12 a.m., Fri. - Sat. 11 a.m. - 1 a.m., Sun. 12 p.m. - 11 a.m.

Tinley Cantonese Restaurant
17747-49 S. Oak Park Ave.
708/532-5390
Most come to this Chinese restaurant for the buffets—Monday through Friday the all-you-can-eat lunch is $5.29 between 11:30 a.m. and 2:30 p.m., Friday and Saturday 5 p.m. - 9 p.m. and Sunday 5 p.m. - 8 p.m. the dinner feast is $7.69. House specialties off the menu include Rainbow Won Ton "just say number 34" ($6.59) and Sweet and Sour Won Ton ($6.59).
Open Mon. - Thurs. 11 a.m. - 9:30 p.m., Fri. 11 a.m. - 10 p.m., Sat. 12 p.m. - 10 p.m., Sun. 3 p.m. - 9:30 p.m.

Jim's Inn
17747-49 S. Oak Park Ave.
708/532-9225
Jim's Inn is an easy going place to kick back with friends, play some pool, and have a burger. Four small booths and a modest menu of hot dogs, hamburgers ($2), and a full slabs of ribs ($10.75) accommodates the eaters at Jim's, while the large winding bar provides plenty of space to sit and enjoy a drink. The pool table area, though, which is larger and roomier than most bars, is the major draw.
Open Mon. - Thurs. 8 a.m. - 2 a.m., Fri. 7 a.m. - 3 p.m., Sat. 8 a.m. - 3 p.m., and Sun. 12 p.m. - 2 a.m.

"World Famous Chops"

Hog Wild
16731 S. Oak Park Ave.
708/614-9440
Hog Wild specializes in pork chops, which means you'll be able to order them almost every way imaginable. A pork chop dinner with fries or oven-browned potatoes and applesauce, coleslaw, or beans for $6.14 or a huge pork chop sandwich with fries and a drink for $5.62 are two compelling choices. If you're laying off the bacon, they also have chicken sandwiches (including one Philly style) and cheeseburgers. Carry your chops out, but if you can't wait until you get home, there's a small dining area where you can eat and run.
Open daily 11 a.m. - 9 p.m.

Olympic Star
7100 W. 171st St.
708/532-8900
I wonder if there is anyone within a 25 miles radius of 7100 W. 171st who has not heard of the Olympic Star or eaten there. Over the years it has become more than a local hang out, it's become an institution. One recent meal found our table with a generous chicken stirfy (per the server's suggestion); the jumbo frankfurter; orzo chicken noodle soup (a big thumbs up); and a pita club stuffed with ham, turkey, bacon, Swiss cheese, lettuce, and tomato. Hands down, though, the chicken melt was the best at the table.
Most items $1.50-$6. Open daily, 24 hours.

Bogart's
17265 Oak Park Ave.
708/532-5592
Bogart's. Bogart's. Bogart's. That's all anyone in Tinley Park talks about—for good reason. If you plan on dining in this Casablanca setting with turban-wearing servers, you better make a reservation. And, after you have that reservation, still plan on waiting a good forty-five minutes to be seated. Those who have dining at Bogart's down to a science tell me the best way to do it is to make your reservation, call at your designated time and ask how long the wait is, and then "bogie" on over.

A life-size, charismatic Bogart embossed in the glass front door greets patrons as they enter. Just inside, the chef is grilling the steaks for everyone to see at an open fire grill and filling the restaurant with terrific aromas. As hungry as the smells make you, try not to eat the plastic steaks which are on display to show customers the size of the different cuts.

Prior to each meal, a relish tray (cottage cheese, beets, cole slaw) and soup (a large crock of French onion with melted cheese) or salad are brought to the table. The steaks are worth the wait, enormous, fairly priced, and in every way live up to their tantalizing aroma. (Even those with above average appetites might want to consider splitting one.)
Open daily 11 a.m. - 11 p.m.

SHOPPING

Tinley Park Tobacco
7943 W. 171st St.
708/532-1850
http://www.tinleyparktobacco.com/
Tinley Park Tobacco's huge, walk-in humidor is one of the largest in the SS at 275 square feet, and their selection of zippo lighters, tobacco, cigars, and accessories is one of the best in the area.
Open Mon. - Sat. 9 a.m. - 8 p.m., Sun. 10 a.m. - 3 p.m.

Door County Candles
The Village Mart Gift Gallery
17040 S. Oak Park Ave.
708/614-1181
This gift gallery is separated into sections for consignors who sell items ranging from handmade crafts to gourmet coffee and candles from Door County. Sections of interest are the Door County candle booth, the stained glass booth, and the "Painted Treasures" booth which features hand-painted bottles, china, and pottery.
Open Tues. - Fri. 10 a.m. - 5:30 p.m., Sat. 10 a.m. - 4 p.m.

The Sensible Resale Shop
Proceeds to Together We Cope
17030 S. Oak Park Ave.
708/633-5040
Together We Cope supports the working poor to insure they do not become homeless when a tragedy strikes. They offer food, clothing, household items, furniture, and school supplies, as well as support and encouragement. Their Sensible Resale Shop sells mostly clothes (business, casual, and winter coats), jewelry, games, and books. Dressing rooms are available. The Together We Cope headquarters is next door and is always looking for volunteers.
Open Mon. & Thurs. 10 a.m. - 7 p.m., Wed. 10 a.m. - 5 p.m., Sat. 10 a.m. - 3 p.m.

LODGING

At the corner of Harlem and 185th is the Northcreek Business Center, a colony of hotels that supports the "industrial corridor"—a particular stretch of I-80 designed to attract businesses and manufacturers with its lower tax rates.

Comfort Suites
18400 Spring Creek Dr.
800/228-5150

Fairfield Inn
18511 North Creek Dr.
708/633-1050

Hampton Inn
18501 North Creek Dr.
708/633-0602
This inn has 64 rooms with either two queen size beds or one king size. They also have an indoor/outdoor pool and whirlpool, color TV with cable, free local calls, a hair dryer, refrigerator, and a safe.

Budgetel Inn
7255 W. 183rd St.
800/800-4-BUDGET
Budgetel maintains 106 rooms (with cable TV, free local calls, coffee makers, and complimentary room-delivered breakfasts) and an indoor/outdoor pool.
Rooms for smokers available.

WILMINGTON

Just The Facts

City of Wilmington
55 miles southwest of Chicago

Contact:
City Hall 708/389-0200

TOURING

You may or may not know that the large man-like statues seen atop restaurants and tobacco shops are called Muffler Men. In the 1960s Muffler Men decorated gas station chains, but as the stations closed, the macho Muffler Men were stripped of their dignity and sold as novelties to other businesses. Visit *http://www.roadsideamerican.com/sct/muffler.com*, a site devoted to Muffler Men sightings. You're pretty sharp, so you've probably already guessed, that one such Muffler Man has made Wilmington, Illinois his home. He is known as the Muffler Spaceman and he nonchalantly stands on the **Launching Pad Restaurant** (810 E. Baltimore, 815/423-5326). His helmet lights up from the inside at night—neat!

RECREATION

Des Plaines Conservation Area
24621 North River Road
815/423-5326
Besides 200 acres of water for fishing, the conservation area has facilities for camping, hiking, hunting, and horseback riding. Forsythe Woods, a nearby forest preserve, provides more hiking trails, cross

country ski paths, pavilions, grills, picnic areas, horseshoe pits, play-fields, fishing, and camping.
Open Jan. - Oct., Nov. - Dec. for hunting only

WORTH

Just The Facts

Worth
20 miles south of Chicago

Access Via:
I-294

TOURING

Holy Sepulchre Cemetery
6001 W. 111th St.
312/445-2022
It is said that people receive miracle cures at Holy Sepulchre Cemetery from the grave of 14-year-old Mary Alice Quinn. Some believe that in life Quinn had the gift of healing and just hasn't stopped working since put in the ground. In addition to receiving cures, visitors of to Mary Alice's gravesite also claim a phantom scent of roses pervades the area.

Also buried here is Richard J. Daley, father of current Chicago mayor Richard M. Daley, who himself was a long-time mayor of the then-corrupt city.

APPENDIX A: PHONE NUMBERS & INTERNET ADDRESSES

Individual Communities

Alsip
Village Hall - 708/385-6902
http://www.lincolnnet.net/communities/alsip/alsip.htm
http://www.villageprofile.com/alsip/

Beecher
Village Hall - 708/946-2261
Public Library - 708/946-9090
Chamber of Comm. - 708/946-3145
http://www.lincolnnet.net/communities/beecher/beecher.htm

Blue Island
City Hall - 708/597-8600
http://www.lincolnnet.net/communities/blueisland/blueisland.htm

Bourbonnais
Village Hall - 815/933-1383

Bradley
Village Hall - 815/933-8533

Braidwood
Mayor's Office - 815/458-2333
Chamber of Comm. - 815/458-6317

Burbank
City Hall - 708/599-5500
http://www.lincolnnet.net/communities/burbank/burbank.htm

Calumet City
Town Hall - 708/891-8100

Chicago Heights
City Hall - 708/756-5307
http://www.lincolnnet.net/users/lmchghts/
Library - 708-754-0323
http://www.sls.lib.il.us/CHS/

Country Club Hills
Village Hall - 708/798-2616
http://www.lincolnnet.net/communities/countryclubhills/countryclubhills.htm
Library - 708/798-5563
http://www.grandeprairie.org/

Crete
Village Hall - 708/672-5431
http://www.lincolnnet.net/users/lmcrete/
http://www.lincolnnet.net/communities/crete/crete.htm

Dolton
Village Hall - 708/798-3000
http://www.thetimesonline.com/communities/dolton/
http://www.lincolnnet.net/communities/dolton/dolton.htm

Evergreen Park
Village Hall - 708/422-1551
http://www.lincolnnet.net/communities/evergreenpark/evergreenpark.htm

Flossmoor
Village Hall - 708/798-2300
http://www.lincolnnet.net/communities/flossmoor/flossmoor.htm
Library - 708/798-4006
http://homepage.interaccess.com/~flssmoor/fpl.html

Ford Heights
Village Hall - 708/758-3131
http://www.lincolnnet.net/communities/fordheights/fordheights.htm

Frankfort
Village Admin. - 815/469-2177
Chamber of Comm. - 815/469-3356
http://www.lincolnnet.net/frankfort.vil/

Glenwood
Village Hall - 708/758-5150
http://www.lincolnnet.net/communities/glenwood/glenwood.htm

Harvey
Library - 708/331-0757
http://www.harvey.lib.il.us/

Hazel Crest
Village Hall - 708/335-9600
Library - 708/798-5563
http://www.grandeprairie.org/

Homewood
Village Hall - 708/798-3000
Library - 708/798-0121
http://homepage.interaccess.com/~homewood/

Joliet
City Hall - 815/724-4000
http://www.lincolnnet.net/communities/joliet/joliet.htm
http://www.htls.lib.il.us/JPB/

Kankakee
http://www.lincolnnet.net/communities/kankakee/kankakee.htm
Library - 815/939-4564
http://www.htls.lib.il.us/KKB/

Lansing
Village Hall - 708/895-7200

Lemont
Village Hall - 630/257-2532
Chamber of Comm. - 630/257-5997
http://www.lemont.il.us/

Lockport
City Hall - 815/838-0549
Chamber of Comm. - 815/838-3557
http://www.lincolnnet.net/communities/lockport/lockport.htm

Manteno
Village Hall - 815/468-8224
http://www.lincolnnet.net/communities/manteno/manteno.htm

Matteson
Village Hall - 708/748-1559
http://www.lincolnnet.net/communities/matteson/matteson.htm

Midlothian
Village Hall - 708/389-0200
http://www.lincolnnet.net/users/lmidloth/template.htm
http://www.lincolnnet.net/communities/midlothian/midlothian.htm

Mokena
Park District - 708/479-1020
Library - 708/479-9663
http://www.htls.lib.il.us/MKB/
http://www.mokena.com

Momence
Village Hall - 815/472-2001
http://www.lincolnnet.net/communities/momence/momence.htm

Monee
Village Hall - 708/534-8301
http://www.lincolnnet.net/communities/monee/monee.htm

New Lenox
Village Info Line - 815/485-7700
Village Hall - 815/485-6452

Oak Forest
Acorn Public Lib. - 708/687-3700
http://www.sls.lib.il.us/ADS/

Oak Lawn
Village Hall - 708/636-4400
http://www.lincolnnet.net/communities/oaklawn/oaklawn.htm
http://www.lincolnnet.net/users/lmoaklwn/
Library - 708/422-4990
http://www.lib.oak-lawn.il.us/

Olympia Fields
Village Hall - 708/503-8000

Orland Park
Village Hall - 708/403-6100
http://www.lincolnnet.net/communities/orlandpark/orlandpark.htm
http://chicago.digitalcity.com/orlandpark/

Park Forest
Village Hall - 708/748-1112
http://www.lincolnnet.net/communities/parkforest/parkforest.htm

Peotone
Village Hall - 708/258-3279
http://www.lincolnnet.net/communities/peotone/peotone.htm

Phoenix
Village Hall - 708/331-2636
http://www.lincolnnet.net/communities/phoenix/phoenix.htm

Plainfield
Village Hall - 815/436-7093
http://www.lincolnnet.net/communities/plainfield/plainfield.htm
Library - 815/436-6639
http://www.htls.lib.il.us/PLB/

Richton Park
Village Hall - 708/481-8950
http://www.lincolnnet.net/communities/richtonpark/richtonpark.htm

Riverdale
Library - 708/841-3311
http://www.sls.lib.il.us/RDS/

Romeoville
Village Hall - 815/886-7200
http://www.lincolnnet.net/communities/romeoville/romeoville.htm

Shorewood
Village Hall - 815/725-2150
http://www.lincolnnet.net/communities/shorewood/shorewood.htm
http://www.htls.lib.il.us/STB/

South Holland
Village Hall - 708/210-2900
http://www.southholland.org/
http://www.lincolnnet.net/communities/southholland/southholland.htm

Tinley Park
Village Hall - 708/532-7700
http://www.ECNet.Net/users/gtinpark/
Library - 708/ 532-0160
http://www.lincolnnet.net/users/lltppl/

University Park
Village Hall - 708/389-0200
Library - 708/534-2580
http://www.lincolnnet.net/users/llunvprk/uplib2.htm

Wilmington
City Hall - 708/389-0200
http://www.lincolnnet.net/communities/wilmington/wilmington/htm

General Regional and Tourism Information

State of Illinois
http://www.state.il.us/

Chicago Southland Convention and Visitors Bureau
http://www.lincolnnet.net/users/lrcscvb/

Illinois Bureau of Tourism
http://www.enjoyillinois.com/

The Illinois and Michigan Canal
http://dnr.state.il.us/i&m/main.htm

Virtual tour of the I&M Canal
http://www.imcanal.org

South Metro Regional Sites

Lincoln Net
http://www.lincolnnet.net

PrairieNet
http://www.prairienet.org

Village Profile
http://www.villageprofile.com

Excite's City Net
http://www.city.net/countries/united_states/illinois/#cities

The Times Online
http://www.thetimesonline.com

Will County
http://www.mcs.net/~willco/

Cook County
http://www.co.cook.il.us/

Kankakee River Valley Community Network
http://www.knet.com/index.html

Roots Web
http://www.rootsweb.com/roots-l/USA/il.html
Great history and genealogy site.

U.S. Speed Traps
http://www.speedtrap.com/us-traps.html

Colleges and Universities

Governors State University
http://www.govst.edu

Joliet Junior College
http://www.joliet.cc.il.us

Lewis University
http://www.lewisu.edu

Moraine Valley Community College
http://www.moraine.cc.il.us

Olivet Nazarene University
http://www.olivet.edu

Prairie State College
http://www.praire.cc.il.us

South Suburban College
http://www.ssc.cc.il.us

St. Xavier University
http://www.sxu.edu

Trinity Christian College
http://www.trnty.com

University of St. Francis
http://www.stfrancis.edu

APPENDIX B: NEWSPAPERS

Beecher Herald
756 Penfield
Beecher, IL 60401
708/946-2151

Bolingbrook Metro Newspaper
1 E. Logan St.
Lemont, IL 60439-3810
708/739-2300

Chicago Tribune Editorial
9220 W. 159th St.
Orland Park, IL 60462-5539
708/349-0598

Crete Record
484 Cass St.
Crete, IL 60417-2956
708/672-8843

Daily Journal
104 W. Main
Peotone, IL 60468
708/258-3410

Daily Journal
8 Dearborn Sq.
Kankakee, IL 60901-3909
815/937-3300

Des Plaines Valley News
6257 S. Archer Ave.
Summit, IL 60501-1718
708/594-9340

The Daily Southtown
7711 W. 159th St.
Tinley Park, IL 60477-1329
708/460-2211

The Daily Southtown
18127 William St.
Lansing, IL 60438-3921
708/821-1200

DIGEST
221 Liberty St.
Morris, IL 60450-2239
815/942-4633

Free Press
111 S. Water St.
Wilmington, IL 60481-1373
815/476-7966

The Herald News
300 Caterpillar Drive
Joliet, IL 60436-1097
815/729-6161

Herald-Morris Daily
1804 Division St.
Morris, IL 60450-1127
815/942-3221

Joliet Times Weekly
214 N. Ottawa St.
Joliet, IL 60432-4007
815/723-0325

Labor Record
724 Railroad St.
Joliet, Il 60436-9524
815/723-3232

Lemont Metropolitan Newspaper
223 Main St.
Lemont, IL 60439-3624
708/257-5300

Lemont Reporter
922 Warner Ave.
Lemont, IL 60439-3955
708/257-1090

Manhattan American
254 Jessie
Manhattan, IL 60442
815/478-3255

MET Newspaper
223 Maint St.
Lemont, IL 60439-3624
708/739-2300

Pendry Labor Publications
1050 N.E. Frontage Rd.
Joliet, IL 60431-8741
815/744-3958

Progress Reporter Press
110 River Rd.
Momence, IL 60954
815/472-4283

Russell Publications
N. First St.
Peotone, IL 60468
708/258-3473

Saint Anne Record
6980 S. State, Rt. 1
Saint Anne, IL 60964-5270
815/427-6734

Shopper
924 E. 162nd St.
South Holland, IL 60473-2442
708/333-5901

Shopper Publications
938 S. State St.
Lockport, IL 60441-3436
815/838-1515

Southtown Ecomonist
54 N. Ottawa St.
Joliet, IL 60432-4345
815/722-7908
http://www.dailysouthtown.com/index/dsindex.html

Star Newspapers
6901 W. 159th St.
Tinley Park, IL 60477
708/802-8800
http://www.starnewspapers.com/index/spindex.html

Taylor Publications
555 S. Schuyler Ave.
Kankakee, IL 60901-5146
815/939-1863

Times
2 River Pl., #-1
Lansing, IL 60438-6028
708/418-2900

Village Newspapers
9540 W. 144th Pl.
Orland Park, IL 60462-2542
708/460-0188

Wilmington Advocate
384 W. Baltimore St.
Wilmington, IL 60481-1291
815/476-7511

Worth Palos Reporter
12247 S. Harlem Av.
Palos Heights, IL 60463-1400
708/448-6161

APPENDIX C: GOLF

Public Golf Courses

Shady Lawn Golf Course
615 S Dixie Hwy
Beecher, IL 60401
708/946-2800

Chicago Hts. Country Club
1100 Scott Ave.
Chicago Heights, IL 60411
708/755-2422

Chicago Hts. Park Golf CRS
315 Glenwood Rd.
Chicago Heights, IL 60411
708/754-3673

Balmoral Woods Ctry. Club
26732 S. Balmoral Woods Dr.
Crete, IL 60417
708/672-7448

Lincoln Oaks Golf Club
390 E. Richton Rd.
Crete, IL 60417
708/672-9401

Longwood Country Club
3503 E. Steger Rd.
Crete, IL 60417
708/758-1811

Tuckaway Golf Club
27641 S. Stoney Island Ave.
Crete, IL 60417
708/946-2259

Green Garden Country Club
9511 W. Manhattan Monee
Frankfort, IL 60423
815/469-3350

Hickory Creek Golf Course
7861 W. Saint Francis Rd.
Frankfort, IL 60423
815/469-1717

Glenwoodie Country Club
193rd & State St.
Glenwood, IL 60425
708/758-1212

Joliet Park District
S. Gougar Rd.
Joliet, IL 60432
815/ 741-7272

Joliet Park District
3200 W. Jefferson St.
Joliet, IL 60431
815/741-7265

Willow Run Golf Course
187th & Maple Rd.
Mokena, IL 60448
815/485-2119

New Lenox Community Park District
485 Marley Rd.
New Lenox, IL 60451
815/462-4653

Indoor Links of America
16356 & 104th Ave.
Orland Park, IL 60467
708/403-4040

Silver Lake Country Club Inc.
147th & 82nd
Orland Park, IL 60462
708/349-6940

Odyssey Golf Course
19110 Ridgeland Ave.
Tinley Park, IL 60477
708/429-7400

White Mountain Rec. Center
9901 W. 179th St.
Tinley Park, IL 60477
708/478-4653

Miniature Golf

Fun Time Square Inc.
11901 S. Cicero Ave.
Alsip, IL 60803
708-388-3500

Hickory Creek Golf Course
7861 W. Saint Francis Rd.
Frankfort, IL 60423
815/469-1717

Coconut Falls Golf & Games
1736 Essington Rd.
Joliet, IL 60435
815/436-6800

Haunted Trails Joliet
1423 N. Broadway St.
Joliet, IL 60435
815/722-7800

White Mountain Recreation Center
9901 179th St.
Tinley Park, IL 60477
708/478-4653

APPENDIX D:
REGIONAL MAPS

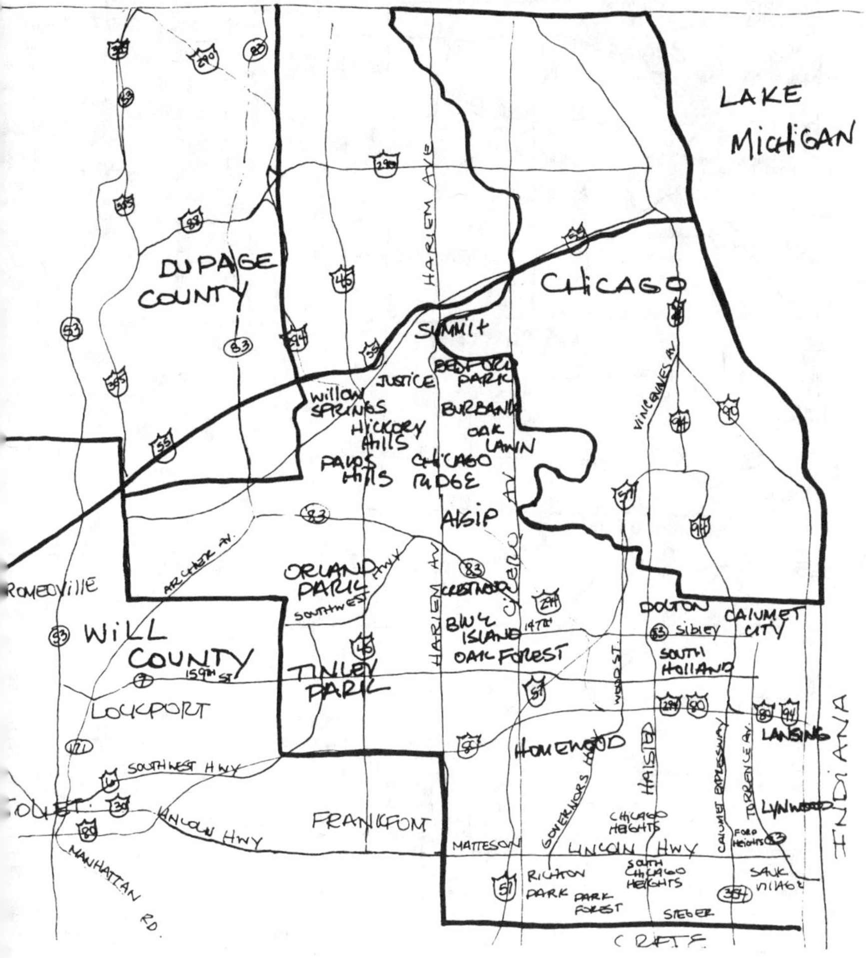

South Suburban Region in Relation to Chicago

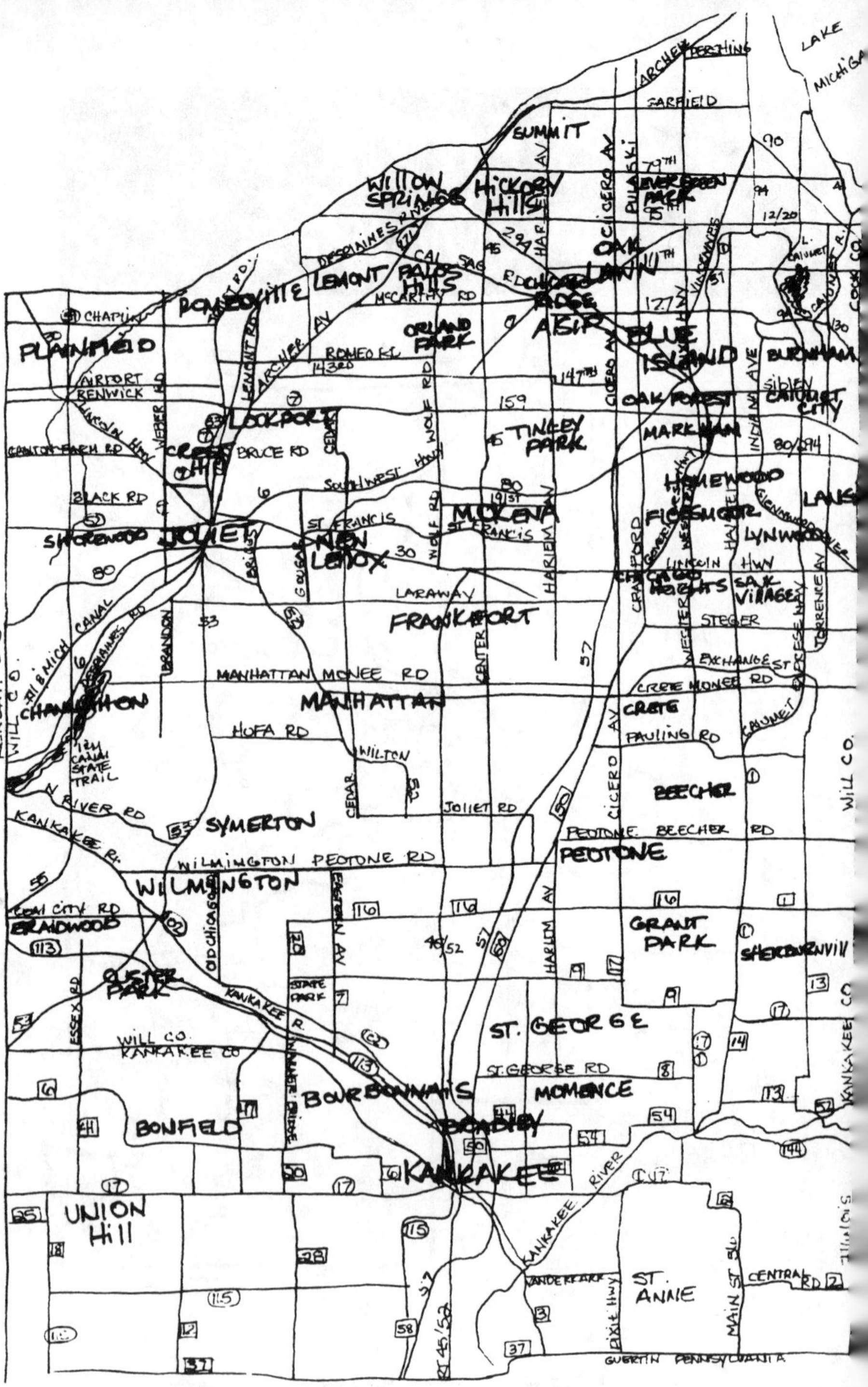

Overview of South Suburban Region

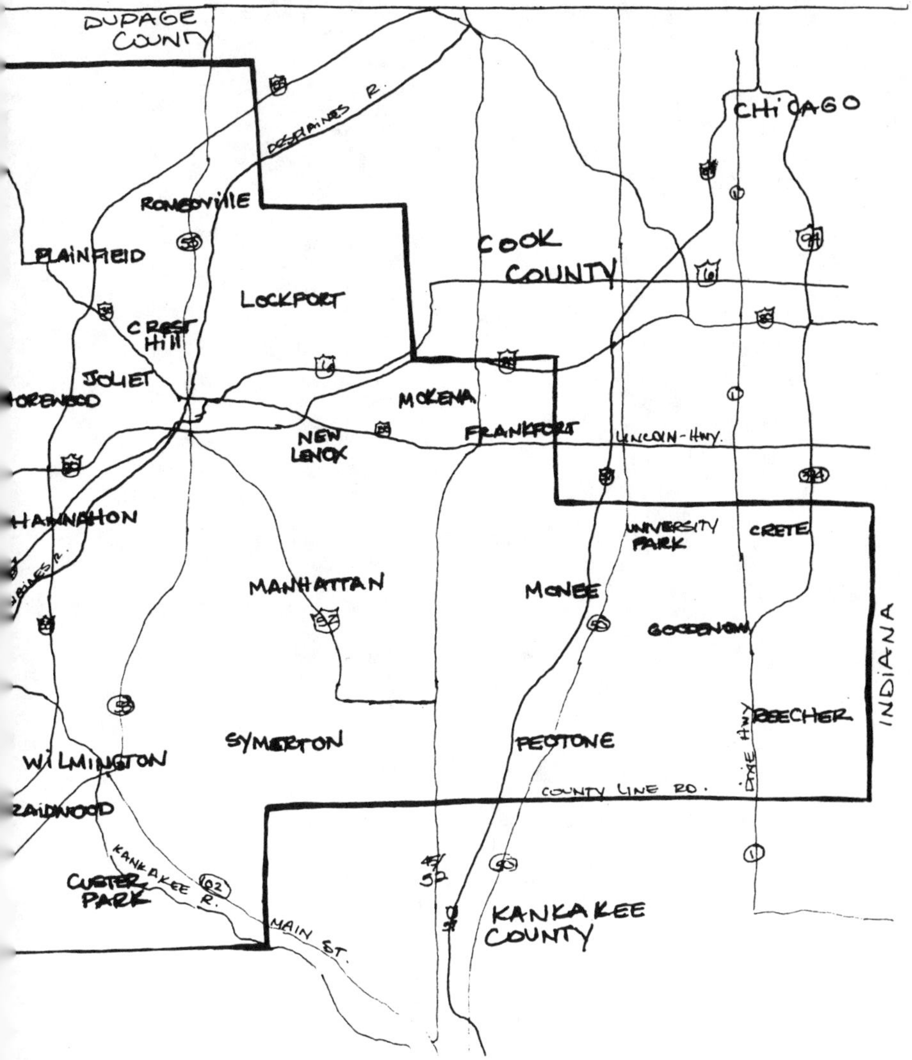

South Suburban Towns in Will County

BIBLIOGRAPHY

Angle, Paul M. and Richard Beyer. *A Handbook of Illinois History.* The Illinois Historical Society, 1943.

Bach, Ira. *A Guide to Chicago's Historic Suburbs.* Chicago: Swallow Press, 1981.

Bergreen, Laurence. *Capone.* New York: Simon & Schuster, 1994.

Bureau of Economic and Business Research. *1996 Illinois Statistical Abstract.*

Campbell, Michelle, "Chicago Heights Seeks Rebirth of 'Glory Days'." *Chicago Sun-Times* (February 27, 1996): 15.

Candeloro, Dominic and Barbara Paul. *Image of America: Chicago Heights.* Chicago Heights: Arcadia Publications, 1998.

Clements, John. *Flying the Colors: Illinois Facts.* 1989.

"Controversy and rejection follow Singer's death." *Lemont Metropolitan* (June 1, 1989).

Cox, Benjamin. "Notes from the Underground." *The Lincoln-way Sun* (January 8, 1998): 24-26.

Crome, Robert. *Illinois Trivia.* Nashville: Rutledge Hill Press, 1992.

Woodruff, George. *Forty Years Ago, the Early History of Joliet and Will County. Vol. 1.* Will Country Historical Society, Summer 1994 (reprint of a lecture delivered at Central Presbyterian Church, Joliet, Illinois, December 17, 1873).

Goldberg, Beverly J. *Profiles II: Economic and Demographic Factbook of Chicago Southland.* Star Newspapers, 1996.

Illinois State Police, Total Offenses Reported, January - September 1997.

"Immigrants, Lincoln support canal completion; Lemont pays tribute to slain president, 1865." *Lemont Metropolitan* (November 24, 1988): 1.

"Indians left elaborate system of overland trails." *Lemont Metropolitan* (May 26, 1998), reprint of map by Albert F. Scharf, 1900.

Johnson, Geoffrey and Dennis Rodkin, "What is Your Home Worth?" *Chicago Magazine* (October 1997): 72-83.

Kappe, Gale, "Following History's Trail." *Chicago Magazine (*April 1987).

Lemont Historic Walking Tour, Lemont area historical society.

"Lockport has a Birthday." Republished by the Will County historical society, (fall 1988): 3, 9.

McClellan, Larry, "Family Wins Second Annual Local History Trivia Quiz." *The Star* (January 25, 1998): A-8.

Michalek, Louise, "Monarch Made Locally." *The Star*, (September 29, 1973): B1-B2.

Noonan, Robert J., "Ah! The Smell of Greasepaint." *Cache* (summer/fall 1991): 7-9.

"100th Anniversary Perpetual Calendar." Chicago Heights Public Library, 1992.

Orr, Elmer F., "Prison at Joliet." *Illinois Lions Magazine* (September 1965): 4-5.

Pleasant Hill Cemetery Record. Frankfort area historical society, South Suburban Genealogical and Historical Society.

Programme. The Historical Pageant of Bloom Township 1833-1933. Chicago Heights

South Suburban Genealogical and Historical Society, "Where the Trails Cross." Vol. 11:3; (spring 1981): 84-87.

South Suburban Genealogical and Historical Society, "Where the Trails Cross." Vol. 11:4; (summer 1981): 143, 125-126, 137-38, 143.

South Suburban Genealogical and Historical Society, "Where the Trails Cross." Vol. 12:2; (winter 1981-82): 49-52, 57.

South Suburban Genealogical and Historical Society, "Where the Trails Cross." Vol. 12:4; (summer 1982): 139-147.

Szucs, Loretto Dennis, *Chicago and Cook County: a guide to research*, Ancestry Section Five, Cemeteries in Metropolitan Chicago area.

"The Hot Air Gang." *Lemont Observer* (1896).

"The I&M Canal 150th Anniversary Guide, 1848-1998." *Chicago Tribune* (1998).

"They Helped to Keep Our Country Free." Will county historical society, (November 1977).

Whiteside, John, "Daring Stateville Escape Happened 39 Years Ago Today." *Herald-News,* Joliet (October 9, 1981).

Zasadny, Julie, "Building on Faith." *Southtown Economist* (February 1, 1998): 1.

INDEX

A

Abe Lincoln Motel, 69
AJ Hot Dogs and Gyros, 159
Alexi's Charhouse and Lounge, 175
All Small, 64
Alsip, 9-11
  History, 9
  Recreation, 10
  Shopping, 10-11
Alsip Nursery, 55-56
Alsip Park District, 9
Alton/Legion Park, 112
Always Open, 53
Amazing Fantasy Books & Comics, 64
Ambrosino's Italian Market and Deli, 60
Annie Lee & Friends Art Gallery, 74
Annual Harvest Fest and Native American Indian Fest, 70
Annual Park Forest Art Fair, 183
Annual Running of the Scenic Ten Mile Run and 5k, 183
Anthony's Pancake House and Restaurant, 126
antiques, 43, 62, 66, 69, 99-100, 117-118, 125-126, 127, 149, 173
Antiques on State, 127
Antique Parlour, 117-118
Antiques Unique, 62-63
arcades, 56, 97, 106, 203
art, 204
  outdoor, 181-182
  fairs, 183
Art Gallery of Park Forest Art Center, 181
Auditorium Building, The, 94
Aurelio's Pizza, 32, 42, 58, 98, 161, 205
Autumn Leaves Books, Inc., 83
AWL European Deli, 116

B

Bachelor's Grove, 140-141
Bakers Interiors, 150
bakeries, 49, 116, 148
Balagio, 79
Balmoral Race Track, 38-39
Balmoral Woods Country Club, 37-38
bars/pubs/taverns, 41, 132-133, 136, 146, 152, 166-167, 174, 187, 196-197, 206, 207
batting cages, 106
bed and breakfasts, 128
Beacon Hill Antique Shop, 173
Beecher, 13-16
  History, 13-14
  Shopping, 16
  Touring, 14-15
Beecher Library, 14
Bella Luna, 82
Bengston Pumpkin Farm, 125
Berry Bargain World, 117, 161
Best Western, 84
bike trails, 15, 21, 124, 145, 158, 174, 202
billiards/pool, 56, 207
Bird Haven Greenhouse and Conservatory, 93
Bird Park, 103-104
birding, 93, 103-104, 177
B.J. McMahon's, 166
Blackberry Harvest Dollhouse Museum Shoppe, 83
Black Smith Shops, 63
Bloom Township High School, 27
Bloomvale Cemetery, 30
Blue Island, 17-19
  Food, 18
  Shopping, 19
boating, 21, 103-104, 151, 153
bocce courts, 179
Bocce's Sports Bar and Grill, 136
Bogart's, 208
Bogart's Charhouse, 80
book stores, 64-65, 83
bowling, 56, 174

Bourbonnais, 20-22
Recreation, 20-22
Brandt Cellars International, 115
Brauhaus, 41-42
breakfast, 31, 40, 56, 73, 80, 104, 115, 126, 175, 205
breweries, 146
Brides in the Attic, 65
brunch, 56, 139, 175, 204
Budgetel Inn, 211
Bultema Produce, 16

C

Cactus Carols, 60
Cafe Magnolia, 99
Cal's Chicken City, USA, 40
Calumet City, 23-24
Shopping, 24
Touring, 23
Camp Erwin, 96
camping, 15, 21, 211-212
Camp Sagawau, 113
Canal House Antiques, 127
Canal Street Collectibles, 117
Candle Cottage, 66
candy, 62, 66-67, 159
canoeing, 21
Capricorn Shop, The, 162
Carlo's Restaurant, 104
Carl Vogt Building, 202
carriage rides, 55
cemeteries, 30, 45, 54, 72, 91, 95-96, 101-102, 111, 135-136, 140-141, 144, 185, 194, 213
casinos, 97
Cherry Hills Golf Country Club
Chicago Heights, 25-35
History, 25-27
Food, 31-33
Shopping, 33-34
Touring, 27-28, 30
Chicago Street Bar and Grill, 98
Chicago Street Mercantile, 99-100
Chippewa Campground, 21
Christmas House Walk, 44
Chuck's Place, 41
churches, 23, 91, 94, 111, 133-134, 144, 157
Chef Klaus Steak and Seafood, 59-60
Ciao's, 133
Civil War Days, 129
coffee, 40, 49, 125-126
Coffee Cottage, Inc., 40
Cog Hill Golf Country Club, 114
comic books, 64
Comfort Suites, 210
Concerts on the Green, 57
conservatories, 93
Continental House of Pancakes, 175
Cookie Jar Museum, 113
Country Club Paintball, 73
Courtyard Bistro, 61
Cozy Corner Restaurant, 205
C.P. Meat Market, 160
crafts,
fairs, 70
retail, 42, 64, 119
Crafty Cow, 64
Creamery, The, 61
Crete, 36-44
Entertainment, 38-39
Food, 40-42
History, 36-37
Shopping, 42-43
Special Events, 44
cross-country skiing trails, 15, 21, 48, 115, 124, 145, 178, 203, 211-212
Cruisin' Night, 69

D

Dave's Kitchen, 81
David's Pasta, 99
Danish Cemetery, 111
delis, 60, 116, 160
Des Plaines Conservation Area, 211-212
Die Bier Stube, 57
Discount Records, 68, 139
Doc Bogey's Golf Range, 158

dolls, 64, 83
Door County Candles, 209
Dreamy Delite, 159
Duo's Nearly Nu Resale Shop, 83

E

Eagle's Nest, 186
Edwin's Tavern, 187
Egg & I, 31
Elliot Cemetery, 135-136
Empress Casino, 97
Enrico's, 58-59
Entertainment,
Crete, 38-39
Frankfort, 57
Glenwood, 73
Joliet, 97-98
Lockport, 125
Mokena, 145-146
New Lenox, 158
Oak Lawn, 166-167
Orland Park, 174
Palos Heights, 178
Park Forest, 181-182
Tinley Park, 204-205
Essence Suites, The, 176
Evergreen Park, 45-46
Food, 45-46
Touring, 45
Evergreen Park Community High School, 46
Ewe & Me, 42

F

Fairfield Inn, 106, 210
Farmhouse Antiques, 149
festivals, 44, 69-70, 128-129, 183
Fire & Spice, 67
Fishing Clinics, 152
Fisherman's Wife, The, 67
fishing, 21, 103-104, 151-152, 153, 174, 203, 211-212
flea markets, 11
Fleckenstein's Bakery, 48-49, 148
Flossmoor, 47-49
History, 47-48
Flossmoor Country Club, 48
Flossamore Italian Market, Inc., 49
Food, ***see also*** restaurants.
Beecher, 15
Blue Island, 18
Chicago Heights, 31-33
Crete, 40-42
Flossmoor, 48-49
Frankfort, 57-62
Glenwood, 73
Harvey, 75
Homewood, 79-81
Joliet, 98-99
Kankakee, 104
Lemont, 115-117
Lockport, 125-127
Matteson, 136-137
Mokena, 146-149
Monee, 158-161
New Lenox, 158-161
Oak Lawn, 167-168
Palos Heights, 177
Park Forest, 182
Peotone, 186-187
South Chicago Heights, 35
Tinley Park, 205-209
Ford Airport Hanger, 105
Ford Heights, 50
forest preserves, 15, 174, 195, 177-178, 202, 211-212
Forest View Farms, 203
Frankfort, 51-70
Entertainment, 57
Food, 57-62
History, 51, 53
Lodging, 69
Recreation, 56
Shopping, 62-68
Special Events, 69-70
Touring, 53-56
Frankfort Annual Car Show and Swap, 69

Frankfort Bowl and Billiards, 56
Frankfort Fall Festival, 70
Frankfort Historical Museum, 53, 55
F.S. Allen Residence, 94
Freehauf Building, 113-114
Fresh Starts Restaurant and Bakery, 48-49
Fuccio's, 187
Fuddruckers, 136-137

G

Gabe's Place, 73
galleries, 66, 74, 105, 122, 181
Gambone's, 206
Gatherings, 43
Gaylord Building, 122
General Store, The, 62
Geri Ann's, 67
Georgios Bar and Grill, Ltd., 175
German United Evangelical Church of St. John's, 144
Gino's Steak House, 75
Glady Fox Museum, 121
Glenwood, 71-74
  Food, 73
  Entertainment, 73
  History, 71
  Shopping, 74
  Touring, 72
Glenwood School for Boys, 72
go-karts, 97, 106, 203
Gold 'N' Chains, 68
golf, 37-38, 48, 56, 106, 114, 157, 158, 169-170, 203-204
  miniature golf, 97, 106, 139, 204
Golf 'n' Dogs, 206
Goodenow Grove Forest Preserve, 15
Goose Lake Prairie State Park, 153
Gould St., 14
Grainery, The, 53
Great Room, The, 65
Green Garden Country Club, 56
grocers/markets, 16, 49, 60, 160

H

H.A. Rathje Mill, 185
Hahne Family House, 132
Hampton Inn, 210
Happiday Resale Mart, 33
Harrah's Joliet Casino, 97-98
Harvey, 75-76
Hattendorf Hotel, 37
Haunted Trails Amusement Park, 97
Haven Street, 157
Henry Gross Home & Harness Shop, 134
Henry Vogt House, 201
Hidden Sledding Hill, 158
hiking/walking, 15, 21, 48, 103-104, 124, 145, 153, 158, 165, 174, 177, 190, 202, 211-212,
historical reenactments, 44, 128-129
History,
  Beecher, 13-14
  Chicago Heights, 25-27
  Crete, 36-37
  Frankfort, 51
  Glenwood, 72
  Homewood, 77-78
  Joliet, 85-88
  Lemont, 107-110
  Lockport, 120-122
  Matteson, 131-132
  Mokena, 143-144
  New Lenox, 155-156
  Oak Lawn, 164-165
  Park Forest, 180
  Steger, 191
  Tinley Park, 199-200
Hog Wild, 207
Holiday Inn, 106, 137
Hollywood Park, 106
Holy Sepulchre Cemetery, 213
Homewood, 77-84
  Food, 79-81
  History, 77-78
  Lodging, 84
  Shopping, 82-84
  Touring, 78-79

Homewood-Flossmoor
Park District, 78
Horseback Campground, 21
horseback riding, 22, 124, 202-203,
211-212
Hostert Log Cabins, The, 172
hotels/motels, 69, 84, 106, 137, 150,
176, 210-211
housewares, 65
Humphrey House, 173
hunting, 21, 153, 211-212

I

ice cream, 61, 66, 67, 159
ice skating, 15, 47, 78, 97, 178
Idlewild Golf Club, 48
Illinois and Michigan Canal
Biking/Walking Path, 124
Illinois Philharmonic Orchestra, 181
Illinois State Penitentiary, The,
Stateville, 94
Illinois Theatre Center, 181
Imagination Station, 145
Indian Burial Mounds, 103
Indian Wheel Co., 43
Inwood Recreation Center, 97
Iron Oaks, 48

J

Jacob Henry Mansion, 90
jet skiing, 153
jewelry, 68
Jim and Becky's Horse and Carriage
Service, 55
Jim's Inn, 207
J.N. Michael's, 136
JoAnn's Hot Dogs & More, 35
John Humphrey Trail, 174
Johnson's Greenhouse, 188
Joliet, 85-100
Entertainment, 97
Food, 98-99
History, 85-88
Recreation, 96-97
Shopping, 99-100
Touring, 88-96
Joliet Area Historical Society, The, 93
Joliet—A Midwest Mosaic, 96
Joliet Public Library, 92
Joliet Township High School, 90
Justice, 101-102
JR's Hot Dogs, 167

K

Kankakee, 103-104
Food, 104
Recreation, 103-104
Touring, 103
Kankakee County Historical
Society Museum, 103
Kankakee River State Park, 20-22
Ken's Guest House, 168

L

Lake Katherine Nature Preserve, 177
Lansing, 105-106
Lodging, 106
Recreation, 106
Touring, 105
La Pergola, 32
Larsen Hobby, 161
Launching Pad Restaurant, 211
Lemont, 107-119
Food, 115-117
History, 107-110
Recreation, 114
Shopping, 117-119
Touring, 110-114
Lemont Historical Society, 109
Lemont House, 116
Lemont Inn, 116-117
Lemont Post Office, The, 112-113

Lemont Village Hall, 113
libraries, 14, 92, 186
Liberty Inn Bead & Breakfast, 128
Lincoln Mall, 137-138
Lincoln Oaks Golf Course, 38
Lincoln-Way Theater Guild, 57
living history, 44, 128-129
Lockport, 120-129
Little Al's, 148
  Food, 125-127
  Entertainment, 125
  History, 120-122
  Lodging, 128
  Recreation, 124
  Shopping, 127
  Special Events, 128-129
  Touring, 122-123
Lockport Gallery, 122
Lodging,
  bed and breakfasts, 128
  Frankfort, 69
  Homewood, 84
  hotels/motels, 69, 84, 106, 137, 150, 176, 210-211
  Lansing, 106
  Lockport, 128
  Matteson, 138-139
  Mokena, 150
  Tinley Park, 210-211
Lotton Art Glass Gallery, 105

M

malls, 24, 137-138, 176
Maloni Tavern, 132-133
Mama Vesuvio East Restaurant, 179
Main Street Antiques Emporium, 118
Maple Tree Inn, 18
marathons, 183
Mario's Tacos, 18
markets/grocers, 16, 49, 60, 160
Mary Todd's, 59
Matteson, 131-139
  Food, 136-137
  History, 131-132
  Lodging, 138-139
  Shopping, 137-138
  Touring, 132-136
Matteson Historical Society, 134
Max's Red Hots, 182
Me and My Sister Craft and Creations, 119
Mia Figliali & Co., 98
Mickadoon's Pub, 174
Midlothian, 140-141
  Touring, 140-141
Midwest Carvers Museum, 189
Midwest Stained Glass Arts and Repair, 19
miniature golf, 97, 106, 139
Mitchell's Frankfort Christmas Corner, 63
Mitchell's Steamboat, 146
Mokena, 143-150
  Entertainment, 145-146
  Food, 146-149
  History, 143-150
  Recreation, 145
  Shopping, 149-150
  Touring, 144
Mokena Sales, 149
Monee, 151-152
  Entertainment, 152
  Recreation, 151
Monee Reservoir, 151
Montiferori's, 115
Moraine Valley Community College Fine & Performing Arts Center, 178
Morris, 153
motels/hotels, 69, 84, 106, 137, 150, 176, 210-211
Motel 8, 150
Mount Glenwood Cemetery, 72
museums, 53, 55, 79, 103, 109, 113, 121, 123, 186, 189
Muffler Men, 211
music,
  classical, 166, 181
  jazz, 98
  outdoor concerts, 57
  piano bar, 98
  retail, 68, 138, 139

venues, 205
Music Store, The, 138
Myles Antiques, 118-119

N

Nancy's Pizzeria, 147
Natalie Interiors and Gallery, 82
Nathan Manilow Sculpture Park, The, 181-182
Natural Choices Health Food, 161
nature centers, 48, 93, 113, 165, 166, 177, 190
New China Buffet, 205
New Lenox, 155-163
Entertainment, 158
Food, 158-160
History, 155-156
Shopping, 161-163
Touring, 156-157
New To You Children's Resale Shop, 68
New World Music Theatre, 205
Nick's Barbecue, 179
Norton Warehouse, 123
Northwoods Saloon, 41
Nortmeir House, The, 133

O

Oak Lawn, 164-168
Entertainment, 166-167
Food, 167-168
History, 164-165
Recreation, 165-166
Touring, 165
Oak Lawn School, 165
Oakwood Cemetery, 91-92
Odyssey Fun World, 203
Odyssey Golf Club & Banquets, 204
Old Bank Antique Shop, The, 173
Old Canal Days, 128-129
Old Plank Road Trail, 145
Old Town Restaurant, 116
Old Zion Landmark, 202
Olympia Fields, 169-170
Olympia Fields Park District, 169-170
Olympic Star, 208
Orland Park, 171-176
Entertainment, 174
Food, 175
Lodging, 176
History, 171
Recreation, 174
Shopping, 176
Touring, 172-173
Orland Park Village Center, 171-172
Orland Square Mall, 176
outdoor concerts, 57, 172
Over the Edge, 152

P

Pacific Tall Ships Co., 114
paintball, 73
Paisano's Pizza, 158
Palos Heights, 177-179
Entertainment, 178
Food, 178-179
Recreation, 177-178
Touring, 177
Papa Geo's Family Restaurant and Pizzeria, 99
Park Forest, 180-183
Entertainment, 181-182
Food, 182
History, 180
Special Events, 183
Touring, 181
parks, 78, 93, 103-104, 112, 153, 165-166, 181-182
Pastime Cafe and Antiques, 125
Peotone, 184-188
History. 184
Food, 186-187
Shopping, 188
Touring, 185-186
Peotone Cemetery, 185
Peotone Historical Museum, 186

Peotone Public Library, 186
Pilcher Park Nature Center, 93
Pioneer Settlement, 123, 128
Pleasant Hill Cemetery, 54
pool/billiards, 56, 207
Potawatomi Campground, 21
Prairie View Gallery, 127
Price is Right Resale Shop, 63
Princess Cafe, 15
Public Landing, 126-127
pumpkin farms, 125

R

race tracks, 38-39
record stores, 68
Recreation,
  Alsip, 9-10
  Bourbonnais, 20-22
  Crete, 37-38
  Flossmoor, 48
  Frankfort, 56
  Joliet, 96-97
  Kankakee, 103-104
  Lansing, 106
  Lemont, 114
  Lithuanian, 116, 117
  Lockport, 124
  Mokena, 145
  Oak Lawn, 165-166
  Palos Heights, 177
  Tinley Park, 202-204
  Wilmington, 211-212
Reilly's Daughter, 167
resale/thrift shops, 33, 63, 68, 83, 138-139
Resurrection Cemetery, 101-102
restaurants,
  American, 35, 41, 59, 60, 61, 73, 80, 81, 104, 116, 125, 126-127, 136, 148, 160, 174, 186, 206, 208,
  bar and grill, 41, 98, 136, 148-149, 175, 196-197
  breakfast, 31, 40, 56, 73, 80, 104, 115, 126, 175, 205
  Bohemian, 116
  brunch, 56, 139, 175, 204
  burgers, 46, 81, 136-137, 160, 207
  cafés, 15, 40, 99, 125-126
  Cajun/New Orleans, 18, 115, 126-127
  chicken, 15, 40, 80, 175, 197
  Chinese, 59, 205, 207
  chops, 80, 197, 207
  coffee, 40, 49, 125-126
  delis, 60, 116, 160
  diners, 62, 205
  fast food, 35, 46, 146, 159, 167, 182
  German, 41-42, 57-58, 116
  Greek, 175
  gyros, 61-62, 80, 146, 159, 160
  hot dogs, 35, 146, 159, 167, 182, 205-206
  Italian, 32, 58, 79, 98, 99, 158, 178-179
  Korean, 116
  Lithuanian, 116, 117
  Mediterranean, 97
  Mexican, 18
  pizza, 32-33, 42, 58-59, 98, 99, 147, 148, 58, 160, 161, 179, 187, 205
  Polish, 116
  ribs, 45, 80, 126, 179, 197, 207
  sandwiches, 40, 41, 59, 80, 148
  seafood, 15, 49, 59-60, 73, 80, 99, 126-127, 139, 197
  steak, 15, 59-60, 75, 80, 99, 126, 139, 147, 208
Rialto Square Theatre, 88-89
Richard D. Irwin Park, 78
riding stables, 22, 203
  trails, 124, 211-212,202-203
Rising Sun, 59
River Oaks Mall, 24
Roll 'n Ribs, 45
Rose Hill Cemetery, 54
Rosewood on the Green, 178
Rosie's Diner, 62
Rusty Nail, 167

S

St. James at Sag Bridge, 110-111
St. John's Cemetery, 144
St. John's School, 90-91
St. Mary Cemetery & Mausoleum, 45
St. Patrick Parish, 91
St. Paul's Evangelical Church, 133-134
St. Peter's Lutheran Church, 91
St. Xavier College, 165
Sanctuary, The, 157
Sanctuary Crystals, 10
Sand Ridge Nature Center, 190
schools, 27, 46, 72, 86, 90, 165
Second Chance II Resale Shop, 33
Sell it Again Sam, 138-139
Sensible Resale Shop, The, 209
Sherwood Inn, 160
Shopping,
  Alsip, 10
  Beecher, 16
  Blue Island, 19
  Calumet City, 24
  Chicago Heights, 33-34
  Crete, 42-43
  Frankfort, 62-68
  Glenwood, 74
  Homewood, 82-84
  Joliet, 99-100
  Lemont, 117-119
  Lockport, 127
  Matteson, 137-138
  Mokena, 149-150
  Orland Park, 176
  Peotone, 188
  Tinley Park, 209-210
Simply Sweets, 159
skiing,
  cross-country trails, 15, 21, 48, 115, 124, 145, 178, 203, 211-212
sledding, 158, 177-178
Smokey Row, 112
South Chicago Heights, 34-35
  Food, 35
South Holland, 189-190
  Recreation, 189
  Touring, 189-190
South Suburban Humane Society, 34
Southwest Symphony Orchestra, 166
Souzy's Drive-In, 46
Special Events,
  Crete, 44
  Frankfort, 69-70
  Lockport, 128
  Park Forest, 183
Spring Creek Preserve, 124
state parks, 20, 153
Steak Alexandria, The, 99
Steger, 191
Storehouse of Knowledge, 68
Strand Cafe, The, 115
Statuary, 163
Surma's Restaurant, 80
Swallow Cliff Sports Area, 177
Swap-O-Rama Flea Market, 10-11

T

Tender Trap, The, 31
Terra Firma, 66, 84
Teryl's Boutique, 43
theater/stage, 57, 88-89, 181
Thorn Creek, 195
Thornton, 193-197
  History, 193-194
  Touring, 194-197
Thornton Quarry, 194-195
Tinley Cantonese Restaurant, 207
Tinley Creek Trail, 174, 202
Tinley Park, 199-210
  Entertainment, 204-205
  Food, 205-209
  History, 199-200
  Lodging, 210
  Recreation, 202-204
  Shopping, 209
  Touring, 200-202
Tinley Park Tobacco, 209
tobogganing, 177-178
Tom's Family Restaurant, 80
Tony's Pizza, 187

Touring,
Beecher, 14-15
Calumet City, 24
Chicago Heights, 27-28, 30
Frankfort, 53-56
Glenwood, 72
Homewood, 78-79
Joliet, 88-96
Kankakee, 103
Lansing, 105
Lemont, 110-114
Lockport, 122-123
Matteson, 132-136
Mokena, 144
Monee, 156-158
New Lenox, 156-158
Oak Lawn, 165
Palos Heights, 177
Park Forest, 181
Peotone, 185-186
Tinley Park, 200-202
Wilmington, 211-212
Worth, 213
Town & Country Fashions, 162-163
trails, 15, 21, 93, 103-104, 124, 145, 153, 158, 165, 174, 177, 202, 212-213
Treat Street, 67
Trinity Gift Shop, The, 162
Trinity Lutheran Church, 157
Trolley Barn, 66
Twin Towers Building, 172-173

U

Union Cemetery, 54
Union Station, 90

V

Van Horne's Cabin, 156
Village Barber Shop, 132
Village Door, The, 84
Village Door Dry Cleaners, 79
Village Pizzeria, 148
virtual reality, 146
Vogt Visual Art Center, 204

W

walking/hiking, 15, 21, 48, 103-104, 124, 145, 153, 158, 165, 174, 177, 190, 202, 211-212,
Washington Square Restaurant, The, 80
water parks, 10
water skiing, 153
Wee Folks Peddlers, 42
wetlands, 166
White Street Gallery & Framing, 66
Widow McCleary's Pub and Grill, 196-197
Wild Food Workshop, 145
Wild West Days, 44
William G. Stratton Park, 153
Will County Courthouse, 91
Will County Fairgrounds, 185
Will-South Cook Soil and Water Conservation District, 163
Wilmington, 211-212
Touring, 211
Recreation, 211-=212
wine stores, 115
World's End, 146
Wolfe Wildlife Wetlands, 166
Worth, 213
Touring, 213

PUBLISHER'S CREDITS

Cover Design by Timothy Kocher.

Interior Design by Sharon Woodhouse, with Timothy Kocher.

Cover Photos by Rames Shrestha and William Arroyo.

Interior Photos by Christina Bultinck.

Maps by Christina Bultinck.

Editing by Brandon Zamora and Sharon Woodhouse.

Proofreading by Brandon Zamora, Susan McNulty, Sharon Woodhouse, and Ken Woodhouse.

Layout by Brandon Zamora and Sharon Woodhouse.

Indexing by Brandon Zamora, Sharon Woodhouse, and Ken Woodhouse.

The text of *A Native's Guide To Chicago's South Suburbs* was set in Times New Roman, with headings in CAC Norm Heavy.

ABOUT THE AUTHORS

Christina Bultinck

Christina Bultinck grew up in Frankfort, Illinois and attended Joliet Junior College before moving to Chicago to study online media at Columbia College. Her time is now split between Chicago's north side and Frankfort, where her parents, brother, two cats, and friends still reside. She feels privileged to have grown up in a small, beautiful, and historic town, and hopes, with the publication of this book, to encourage others to learn about their local history

Bultinck's articles have appeared in major trade, popular, and online magazine. In 1996 Christina started InfoKey, a research company that specializes in Internet research, online media, and monitoring trends in the industry, and for which she has written *The Recruiter's Bible*. Since then, the majority of her writing has been technical and reference-oriented though her first love is, and always will be, comedy.

When she's not obsessing about history she's collecting it. Coins, old books, 78-rpm records, and stock certificates are her favorite pieces of history to hold. In addition to antiquing, she spends her free time reading and trying, with no luck, to get the hang of swing dancing.

Christy Johnston-Czarnecki

Christy Johnston-Czarnecki was born in Chicago, but makes her home in the South Suburbs. She has lived in Blue Island and Frankfort, where she spent her grade school and high school years. She now resides in the suburb of Peotone with her husband and daughter. After receiving her bachelor's degree in literature and library science from Western Illinois University, she spent some years as a children's librarian with the Mokena Public Library District.

Christy's love for the South Suburbs runs deep, which made writing this book a bit of a love story. To those who are unfamiliar with the area she says, "You don't know what you're missing."

When she is not chasing around after her daughter, Christy loves to read, write poetry, and make crafts. Most importantly, she has never missed an episode of *90210*.

LAKE CLAREMONT PRESS FAVORITES

Chicago Haunts: Ghostlore of the Windy City (Revised Edition)
by Ursula Bielski
From ruthless gangsters to restless mail order kings, from the Fort Dearborn Massacre to the St. Valentine's Day Massacre, the phantom remains of the passionate people and volatile events of Chicago history have made the Second City second to none in the annals of American ghostlore. Bielski captures over 160 years of this haunted history with her unique blend of lively storytelling, in-depth historical research, exlcusive interviews, and insights from parapsychology. Called "a masterpiece of the genre," "a must-read," and "an absolutely first-rate-book" by reviewers, *Chicago Haunts* continues to earn the praise of critics and readers alike.
0-9642426-7-2, softcover, 29 photos, $15

Hollywood on Lake Michigan:
100 Years of Chicago and the Movies
by Arnie Bernstein
This engaging history and street guide finally gives Chicago and Chicagoans their due for their prominent role in moviemaking history, from the silent era to the present. With trivia, special articles, historic and contemporary photos, film profiles, anecdotes, and exclusive interviews with dozens of personalities, including Studs Terkel, Roger Ebert, Gene Siskel, Dennis Franz, Harold Ramis, Joe Mantegna, Bill Kurtis, Irma Hall, and Tim Kazurinsky. Foreword by *Soul Food* writer/director, George Tillman, Jr.
0-9642426-2-1, softcover, over 80 photos and graphics, $15

Know More, Spend Less:
A Native's Guide To Chicago, 3rd Edition
by Sharon Woodhouse,
with expanded South Side coverage by Mary McNulty
Venture into the nooks and crannies of everyday Chicago with this unique, comprehensive budget guide. Over 400 pages of free, inexpensive, and unusual things to do in the Windy City make this the perfect resource for tourists, business travelers, visiting suburbanites, and resident Chicagoans.
0-9642426-0-5, softcover, photos, maps, $12.95

ORDER FORM

Please send me autographed copies of the following Lake Claremont Press titles:

A Native's Guide to Chicago, 3rd Ed.	_______ @ $12.95 =	__________
A Native's Guide To Chicago's South Suburbs	_______ @ $12.95 =	__________
A Native's Guide To Chicago's Northern Suburbs	_______ @ $12.95 =	__________
A Native's Guide To Chicago's Western Suburbs	_______ @ $12.95 =	__________
A Native's Guide To Chicago's Northwest Suburbs	_______ @ $12.95 =	__________
Chicago Haunts: Ghostlore of the Windy City, Revised Ed.	_______ @ $15.00 =	__________
Hollywood on Lake Michigan: 100 Years of Chicago & The Movies	_______ @ $15.00 =	__________

Discounts when you order multiple copies!

2 books—10% off total
3-4 books —20% off total
5-9 books—25% off total
10+ books—40% off total

Shipping Fees

$2 for the first book and $.50 for each additional book or a maximum of $5.

Subtotal: __________

Less Discount: __________

New Subtotal: __________

8.75% tax for Illinois Residents: __________

Shipping: __________

TOTAL: __________

Name____

Address____

City________________________**STATE**__________**ZIP**______________

Enclose check, money order, or credit card number.

Visa/Mastercard#_____________________________**Exp.** __________

Signature____

Lake Claremont Press
P.O. Box 25291
Chicago, IL 60625
773/784-7517, 784-6504 (fx)

Order by mail, phone, fax, or e-mail.
All of our books have a no-hassle, 100% money back guarantee.

MORE CHICAGO BOOKS FROM LAKE CLAREMONT PRESS

Know More, Spend Less: A Native's Guide To Chicago, 3rd Edition
by Sharon Woodhouse
with expanded South Side coverage by Mary McNulty

A Native's Guide To Chicago's Northern Suburbs
by Jason Fargo

A Native's Guide To Chicago's Western Suburbs
by Laura Mazzuca Toops and John Toops

A Native's Guide To Chicago's Northwest Suburbs
by Martin Bartels

Chicago Haunts: Ghostlore of the Windy City
by Ursula Bielski

Hollywood on Lake Michigan: 100 Years of Chicago and the Movies
by Arnie Bernstein

COMING SOON

Graveyards of Chicago
by Matt Hucke and Ursula Bielski

Chicago Resource Guide for the Chronically Ill and Disabled
by Susan McNulty

Literary Chicago: A Book Lover's Tour of the Windy City
by Gregory Holden